Fi

Your Road Map To Transformational ~~ /ity
by Nicole White

 "Hope" is the thing with feathers -
That perches in the soul -
And sings the tune without the words -
And never stops - at all."
— Emily Dickinson

Special FREE Bonus Gift For You
To help you achieve more success, there are
FREE Bonus Resources for you at:
www.NicoleWhiteWellness.com

www.NicoleWhiteWellness.com

Copyright

Copyright © 2023 Nicole L. White
ALL RIGHTS RESERVED. No part of this book may be reproduced, distributed, or transmitted in any form.

No part of this book may be reproduced or transmitted in any form or by any means, electronic or mechanical, including photocopying, recording, or by any informational storage or retrieval system without permission from the publisher.

DISCLAIMER AND LEGAL NOTICES
The information presented in this book is intended for general knowledge and informational purposes only. It is not a substitute for professional expertise or tailored advice. Readers are encouraged to seek the guidance of relevant professionals or experts for advice specific to their individual needs or circumstances. The author and publisher do not assume responsibility for any consequences, direct or indirect, arising from the use or application of information contained in this book. Additionally, the content may not reflect the most current developments or research in the field. Readers are advised to verify information and consult appropriate professionals for the latest insights.

While all attempts have been made to verify the information provided in this book, neither the author or the publisher assumes any responsibility for errors, inaccuracies, or omissions. The information in this book is provided for general informational and educational purposes only and is not a substitute for professional advice. The author and publisher are not liable for any actions taken based on the information provided.

Editorial and Graphic Support: Ayu Othman, Editorial Support: Michael Harkavy, Cover Design: Alyssa Schifano, Interior Design: Nicole White

ISBN: 978-0-9909816-6-4
LCCN: Library of Congress: 2024900210
For permission requests, write to the author at
Nicole White Wellness
PO Box #1523, Socorro, NM 87801
Nicole@NicoleWhiteWellness.com

What Others Are Saying About Nicole White & Finding Your Angel

"In her profound exploration of the timeless concept of angels, Nicole brings forth a remarkable sense of cohesion and soulful purpose. Drawing from various traditions, beliefs, and practices she weaves together a tapestry of understanding, illuminating the essence of angels and their significance.

Within the pages of "Finding Your Angel," Nicole gently guides the reader, effortlessly connecting these celestial beings to our intuitive knowing and higher purpose. Through her insightful words, she bestows clarity and meaning upon angels, transforming them into spiritual anchors and guiding forces in our lives.

This book is not only a treasure for those seeking soulful nourishment, but also a source of profound inspiration for anyone on a journey of expansion. It is a perfect selection for book clubs, inviting deep conversations and shared insights. Personally, the wisdom, soulfulness, and encouragement I gleaned from "Finding Your Angel" have become an indelible part of my being.

As I closed the final pages, I found myself uplifted, filled with hope, and overflowing with gratitude for the path that lies ahead. Without a doubt, "Finding Your Angel" is an essential read that will touch your heart and illuminate your spirit."
— Dewey Taylor, Filmmaker, Author, Coach

"The role of angels has been prominent and inspirational over the course of thousands of years of human history. The new book by Nicole White, Finding Your Angel, embraces the historic essence of angels and presents these spirits from a new and compelling perspective. The driving theme of the book is an introspective journey of discovery that summons "your angel" to support the challenges that we all face in our individual paths. The book is replete with scenarios that every reader will easily recognize and creative solutions for communicating with "your angel." Chapters that address the "journey within, creativity, self-love, mindfulness, the unknown, humor, and much more."

"Nicole White's career has been in service to those individuals who search for a more meaningful path and purpose. Finding Your Angel is a crowning achievement in her body of work."
— **Michael Harkavy, Author, Poet**

"This book is a fun read. It is full of tips for charging your creativity in art projects and other aspects of life. It provides insights into the creative process as well as interesting techniques to get started, find your voice, and get into "the zone" for work sessions. Included are tips to overcome painters block, overcome fear of imperfection, and to enhance your work through exploring new techniques. Further, she discusses methods for looking outside yourself for inspiration in creative problem solving (in art and life in general) and finding gratitude and peace. In her words Finding Your Angels (whether real or metaphorical) for guidance.

A section of the book that struck a chord with me has to do with preteens discovering possibilities open to them that may launch them into pursuits of their own direction. It reminded me of one boring summer my mom suggested I read a big book on my own, not required by school, and my discovering wow, reading is really neat (Gone With the Wind). This of course led to more books and curiosity that inspired me to take all the "hard" courses in school to possibly qualify for med school. And while life may take one in different directions, you learn that you are capable and can make things happen.

Perhaps a better example, my own daughter really wanted to travel to Europe solo after high school. I didn't have money to finance such a trip; and while she was experienced in navigating airports solo to stay with her dad, and our family had lived in Europe a bit, I was nervous about the idea. I suggested if she could earn the money, fully plan the trip, make reservations, renew her passport, etc. I would agree to the trip. She accomplished all this and had a successful trip of several months. The power of imagining you can do something and finding courage to try cannot be underestimated. Kids, with a little encouragement and direction (from parents and angels?), can catch fire with ideas and courage that might surprise themselves and you.

When I first started Nicole's "You Can Paint" series, it had been some years since I had painted and it was with some trepidation that I approached "The Dot" exercises, blending complementary colors...a seemingly simple beginning. I still use the dots today to loosen up when I get stuck and have also created a lot of the little birdie paintings as greeting cards for friends. Those classes have provided a focus and time and space and encouragement to actually start painting again. This book supports that focus.

A lot of us older folks who may have held in the back of their minds for years a wish to venture out or try arts or other pursuits sometimes need a little push or acknowledgment that your ideas matter. You are never too old to catch on fire. This book provides encouragement and goal setting to get started. Included are fun stories of Nicole's (and other's) life experiences and how her angels guide her. And finally, she includes creative exercises certainly worth trying. I highly recommend this book." — **L. Mueller, Aspiring Artist from Nicole's "You CAN Paint" series**

"This is a powerful and uplifting read for discovering my soul, body, and mind's wellbeing direction. 'Finding My Angel' is an organized recipe for uncovering my 'WHY' and staying on that path without judgment. The exercises at the end of the chapters inspired me with diverse perspectives and tools to enhance creativity in my life. Nicole provides unwavering support, hope, and love throughout the book. It felt as if Nicole was speaking directly to me. Her boundless creativity and life knowledge are both endless and contagious. This book helped me explore multiple creative solutions for living my life with more authenticity and confidence. I'm now grateful for the imperfections in my life. I'm practicing having a 'beginner's mindset' in both creativity and life. 'Finding My Angel' has become an integral part of my daily routine. If you've ever considered getting a life or creativity coach, read this book. With deep gratitude for Nicole." — **Kat C., Beginner Artist in Nicole's Art Therapeutics and 'You CAN Paint' classes.**

What Others Are Saying About Nicole White & RTT, Rapid Transformational Therapy, Hypnotherapy

"I've always dealt with Generalized Anxiety, and it affects me by making me overthink certain situations and take the joy out of life. I was looking for therapy that lessened the anxiety to improve the quality of my life. The Hypnotherapy session with Nicole was a little anxiety producing at first, but then I settled down and let the process play out. Almost overnight (after the session) I started feeling calmer during work interactions, and was able to take my time responding to anxious people, so that I didn't reflect their own anxiety. I feel much more centered now, as long as I continue to do the work, and recommend Nicole to anyone dealing with panic attacks or anxiety that interferes with one's life." — **Keith, Business Owner, Virginia**

"After having just one session with her I truly feel like a new person. I had no idea that things that happened in my childhood were affecting me so much today. I highly recommend Nicole to help you discover what is keeping you from living an amazing and fulfilled life!!!" — **Ana, MI**

"I had a paralyzing and unexplainable fear of moving forward into public speaking in my career as an author and a coach. The RTT session helped me to understand the deeply embedded causes of this fear. Two weeks later, the dread and fear have been replaced by confidence and joy and I have been able to move forward. I highly recommend working with Nicole!" — **Ruth Sandoval, MA, BCC, Intuitive Life Coach, Author, Albuquerque, NM**

"Nicole, I just have to tell you that I am so grateful for our session together! I was able to release some of my issues and feel so much lighter now. The recording was amazing and I anticipate listening to it every day now. Thank you so much! You are talented!"
— **Denise, fellow RTT Practitioner**

"There is a saying that every coach needs a coach, and Nicole is one the best coaches I know. She has helped me by dialing into the root of my situation and provided me with the tools I needed to overcome my subconscious thought process."
— **Melise Thompson, Holistic Health Coach, Kansas, USA**

"During the session with Nicole, I was surprised at the memories from my childhood that came to me that could very possibly be underlying events that made me feel like I didn't belong or was not good enough. Nicole was very professional, but has an essence about her that made me feel safe. At my last business networking mixer, I noticed I felt more at ease and was able to engage in conversation with people more easily and felt like I really fit in."
— **Gina B, Phoenix, AZ**

"I was blown away by my session with Nicole! I was surprised to discover that the way I have been responding to those memories has been from the emotional age of my much younger self and has actually been manifesting as health issues. This new knowledge, in itself, has helped me to realize that I can notice my emotional reactions to current experiences in my life and really put them into perspective, changing my inner dialogue so that I am not holding onto them in a harmful way. The session created a major breakthrough for me. I am grateful for this powerful experience with Nicole". — **Patty Sandoval, Colorado**

"My experience working with Nicole has been powerful and transformative. I was able to release a great deal of anger and resentment I've been carrying with me for so long and begin to finally heal from it and move on. I love listening to my recordings which have become empowering meditations at the end of my day. Thank you for your kindness and light." — **Nikki, California**

"Since my session, I have left my toxic relationship of 13 years!!…it wasn't easy, has not been easy, nor will it be for a while, but I feel so empowered by finally honoring what I know is right for me. Nicole made me feel comfortable, safe, and heard. The RTT session has truly been a turning point in my life and I would highly recommend Nicole for whatever problem you are seeking answers to."
— **Nioma, Canada**

"Nicole helped me with what has been one of my biggest challenges to overcome, a lifelong sugar habit. After one RTT session and a couple of follow-up calls, I am thrilled to say I have yet to touch sugar and now am finding it unappealing. As I am writing this, I am looking at the menu of my favorite local world class bakery, and none of the sweet things are calling my name and creating a craving! It's been one month now of listening every night to the recording Nicole gave and working on "upgrading" food choices, yet still having what I want to eat. Thank you, Nicole, for doing the work you do!" — **Kerry Lee, Artist**

"The stress was killing me and I couldn't take it anymore...I found Nicole White as a local practitioner. She has changed me drastically and quickly. I feel tremendously better and the stress is draining off of me on a daily basis and it's only going to get better and better"
— **Bill Jung, Albuquerque NM**

"I'm completely different after just one session! I used to come home and check-out and now I spend my evenings doing productive things and spending quality time with my family! I had a bad habit that Nicole freed me of in just one session!"
— **Karen Boise, Albuquerque, NM**

> "It's impossible," said pride.
> "It's risky," said experience.
> "It's pointless," said reason.
> "Give it a try," whispered the heart.
> — **Unknown**

For Video Testimonials: www.NicoleWhiteWellness.com
View My Calendar and Book your FREE Discovery Session Today!

What Women Are Saying About Nicole White & Art Therapeutics

Nicole White's Art Therapeutics program is a life changing opportunity.

"I struggle with several health conditions, stress and not taking enough time for my creativity. I participated in the 12-week Art Therapeutics class, and it gave me many tools for inserting creativity into my day, relieving stress, and adding relaxation as part of my daily life. Throughout these discussions and activities, I created a journal that has become part of my creative life. As a result, I am less stressed and more creative than ever. If I get stuck or I need some inspiration, I pull out the journal from the class and I have all kinds of ideas and tools to help me move forward. I can highly recommend the Art Therapeutics program and Nicole White as a creativity coach! I look forward to my weekly sessions, to learn something new as well as to feel supported as I move through my creative journey." — **Denise B.**

What People Are Saying About Nicole White & The You CAN Paint! Community!

"I am very grateful for all I have learned from you, one of which is that if I am in the flow, creativity can happen in countless ways. I feel like I have been since I started working with you, and cannot believe how much has changed since I joined your group."
— **Caren Waters, You CAN Paint Community Member**

"This 5-day on-line watercolor painting challenge has been a great jump start for me to just get going on back-burner painting ideas. Also invaluable is meeting other timid painters and seeing their progress and the uniqueness of their work. If you have ever stood before a blank canvas in angst, thinking what do I do now, I highly recommend getting your brush wet in this short-course."
— **Linda M.**

"YES! You truly can find a few minutes a day to paint and begin to believe in your artistic talents. A community of laughter, questions, enthusiasm and the joy of sharing just one hour a day for 5 days was amazing and just the right push to move me to paint! Nicole is an exceptional guide into a world of watercolor. Her knowledge, energy, belief in our inherent creative talents and encouragement was boundless. I loved every minute and every hour! And, yes, I do continue to paint!" — **Jean S.**

"You have the loveliest heart and teaching style. I'm so happy to have met you!" — **Pamela W.**

"I think I found my niche! And I love your ideas! Thank you!" — **Valerie S.**

"Loved your audio from tonight's class! Thank you for your wonderful and very heartfelt encouragement to all of us! It made a difference." — **Marjorie K.**

"Had so much fun! I am moving towards not judging self too! Love the videos, easy to understand!" — **Kathleen C.**

"My takeaways are many! It was FUN! I'm so surprised I could even do this. I Loved seeing and hearing everyone's work and their thoughts and experiences! And always your amazing teachings. You have a gift and I'm so grateful to be in this group." — **Julie T.**

"Thanks for a wonderful class, Nicole. It has awakened many little brain cells! As a bonus my Sister-in-law and I are going to Zoom from now on instead of talk on the phone so that we can support one another with our art works." — **Adele F.**

"So many thanks for a great series of painless, fun learning. My world has become richer and my goals loftier, but seem to be doable at this point. For that I am grateful. The "I can't paint" bugaboo seems to have become a faint voice off in the distance, easy to ignore." — **Barbara M.**

"Nicole's 5-day painting challenge helped me return to the joy of IRL ("in real life", not digital) painting and discovering how cool watercolors are. She creates a wonderful safe, encouraging, and fun space for everyone to be creative and offers all kinds of great insights and tips on art materials and techniques for every level to help you express yourself through art. I am amazed at all the fantastic instructional and inspirational videos and instructional content she created as part of the course offerings, and it's a treat to watch along while I paint. For those who struggle with feeling 'judged' by their art or have had art instruction/classes that made you feel like you could never paint/draw/be creative, please try out Nicole White's art courses as a way to unlock your own creativity. Everyone has creative potential." — **Ayu O.**

"Nicole's gentle and openhearted expression guides each of the participants into the shallows of the creative process. First getting our feet wet within the creative streams of color and then encouraging each of us to wade deeper and deeper into our own painting journey, until we are at one with our inner child at play. Nicole brings her joy and enthusiasm for life into the creative process and creates a safe space for all to explore. I highly recommend, "The You Can Paint Challenge" and the many other classes Nicole offers. Go ahead! Jump into the pool of your creative unknowns. I guarantee, you will emerge from this process with a new appreciation and perception of your creative self! This experience is not only a healing remedy for the timid or vulnerable artist living within you, but, it's good medicine for your soul!"
— **Kim Rothrock - "From my simple circle of color emerged a Soul Bird."**

Book your FREE Discovery Session Today at www.NicoleWhiteWellness.com

Motivate & Inspire Others
Share This Book!

Retail $24.95

Special Quantity	
5-20 Books	$21.95
21-99 Books	$19.95
100-499 Books	$17.95
500-999 Books	$15.95
1000+ Books	$13.95

To Place An Order Contact:

Nicole White

Nicole@NicoleWhiteWellness.com

www.NicoleWhiteWellness.com

The Ideal Professional Speaker For Your Next Event!

Any organization that wants to develop their people to become "extraordinary," needs to hire Nicole White for a keynote and/or workshop training!

To Contact Or Book

Nicole White, CHt, RTT

TO SPEAK:

Nicole@NicoleWhiteWellness.com

The Ideal Transformational Creativity Coach and Rapid Transformational Therapy Hypnotherapist For You!

If you're ready to overcome challenges, have major breakthroughs, and achieve higher levels, then you will love having Nicole White as your practitioner!

To Contact

Book Your FREE Discovery Call at www.NicoleWhiteWellness.com

Dedication

To Mom & Dad

We didn't always have it easy, but as a family,
we figured things out. For you, I'm grateful that
you never gave up on me, and for that,
I will never give up on you!

To Eric T.

Thank you for the love, laughs, the adventures, and
for always keeping me on high alert! I appreciate your
patience and support of this book and for constantly
asking me "Is it done yet???"

This book is also dedicated to all of my past, future, and current clients and community members. Thank you for traveling this journey with me. Whether our paths cross once or multiple times, I'm forever thankful for the lessons you have taught me and all that we have experienced together!

"Don't Stop Believing"
— Journey

A Very Special Thank You to those who took an early look at this book and provided amazing feedback.

Thank you, Michael Harkavy, Ayu Othman, Dewey Taylor, Kim Henkel, Laura Blaylock, Denise B., Kat C, Linda M., and Mom!

I'm so Grateful for You!

The Mission
Finding Your Angel

The Mission of Finding Your Angel is to empower you in this vibrant chapter of life guiding you to unlock your creative abilities and transform your life. Finding Your Angel is a research-based companion on the path to breaking free from self-imposed limits and discovering ways to cultivate creativity, through simple and fun Creative Practices. This formula aims to assist you in managing stress, releasing depression and anxiety, and embracing a more fulfilled, connected, and creative life.

Together let's venture on a journey that celebrates the wisdom and strength of the Angels by embracing an inspired and creative life. *Finding Your Angel* is here to be a support system and an endless source of inspiration. It's a fast, fun, and welcoming way to navigate the landscape of self-enrichment through Transformational Creativity!

So, join us and be part of this Transformational Creativity Revolution!

All proceeds of this book contribute to a scholarship fund providing support for individuals who may not have the financial means to access the Finding Your Angel Live/Online Program. Your support not only enriches your own journey but also extends a helping hand to those who might not otherwise have the means to experience the program.

Thank you sincerely for your generous support!

A Message To You

"If you want to find the secrets of the universe, think in terms of energy, frequency, and vibration." — Nikola Tesla

Ever wondered if you have An Angel looking out for you? Well, this book is here to show you that you do!

Finding Your Angel will be your companion, showing you how to connect with Your Angel and receive their guidance through research-based creativity practices such as talking out loud, writing, doodling, collages, and simple everyday mindfulness practices.

Think of this book as a friendly reminder that you're never alone in this world. Angels are all around you, and they're here to support and assist you every single day.

Now, you might be thinking, "But I can't see Angels." That's okay – most of us can't either. But that's precisely why you can learn to draw, paint, talk to, and write to them – to remind yourself that they are REAL! **Angels are here for all of us, and they are especially here for you!**

The reason this book came into existence is simple. Like many of you, I've experienced feeling anxious, having panic attacks, and feeling lost and alone in this world. Whether it's been labeled as depression, anxiety, or stress, we've all been there.

This Finding Your Angel book is essential because it equips you with a formula to ground yourself quickly. It provides answers and relief, allowing you to live your best life here on Earth.

Based on research, these Creative Practices can lift you up during the toughest of times and provide solace when you're feeling lost, lonely, or even hopeless. The Angels empower you to take consistent creative action, no matter how small.

I'll be the first to admit that I am a muggle and still struggle, but I no longer succumb to weeks or months of deep depression, or out-of-control anxiety or panic attacks.

I use these exact formulas to find happiness and joy in the little things, helping me remain grateful and hopeful each and every day.

I understand the drowning grips of depression and anxiety. Through a multitude of evidence-based modalities including the practices I share in this book, in my online Art Therapeutics Community, and with Transformational Hypnotherapy, I am, for the most part, a balanced and happy person. Over the past few years, I attribute all of my coping skills to the practices I will share with you in this book.

As you journey into the pages, you'll discover how to Find Your Angel by Asking Your Angel for help and guidance, while embracing the creative practices that resonate with you. These fast-start road maps will remove barriers and bring you a sense of well-being and creative freedom. It's as simple as asking for what you want and what you need.

Feeling off? Experiencing pain, anger, depression, or agitation? Consider it a wake-up call, a reminder that you're veering off course. In those moments, you will learn to lean on Your Angel for connection and guidance. Your Angel will never tire of you, and your requests are never too much. You'll also learn the secrets to unlocking clear communication with Your Angel!

"In a dark place, we find ourselves, and a little more knowledge lights our way." — Yoda

So, as we journey through this book together, you'll discover how creativity can be a powerful tool for enhancing your mental and physical well-being. You'll discover how to bring Your Angel and creativity into your daily life, and together let's embrace the magical powers of creativity for healing, transformation, and personal fulfillment.

You are the director of your story, embrace your own pace, take what resonates with you, and leave behind what doesn't.

Together, we'll navigate the tapestry of Your Angel's wisdom, unlocking your creative forces and inviting in what just might seem like miracles into your life.

May this journey bring you inspiration, healing, and a profound life-long connection to Your Angel and Creativity! Let the pages of this book become your compass, guiding you through understanding and weaving your way into creative dances and illuminating your path to your highest and most fulfilled self.

Are you ready? Your Angel Adventure Awaits…

> Angels are all around us, all the time, in the very air we breathe.
>
> — *Eileen Elias Freeman*

Creativity Is A Dance; it's a space and place that prompts you to take action. This space is designed to encourage specific creative involvement, such as writing and drawing, when you engage with it. Even when every aspect of my life had to fit into my car, there was always a sketchbook handy, creating a space for thinking, capturing, and creating. There's no waiting for the perfect place or time to create; you must CREATE for that perfect space and time to emerge! You are in its forward motion, calling it to you by engaging in the creative dance now.

Table of Contents

Chapter 1
The Origins Of Angels — 1

   Angels Are Always Present — 1
   The Gifts of Angels — 3

Chapter 2
Belief Like A Feather — 9

   Dumbo — 9
   So… What Are Angels? — 10
   Why Believe? — 11
   What is Essential to Believe? — 12

Chapter 3
I Think I Can — 17

   The Little Engine That Could — 17
   Your Angel & Repetition — 18
   What Do I Call My Angel? — 20
   Thank You, Thank You, Thank You! — 23

Chapter 4
Finding The Middle Ground — 27

   Does It Have To Be All-Or-Nothing? — 27
   Changing The All-Or-Nothing Mindset — 31

Chapter 5
Curiosità — 41

   Obstacle Course — 41
   Adopting A Beginner's Mind — 42
   I Wonder… — 44
   Get Curious — 49

Chapter 6
There Is A Voice Inside Of You   55

    Finding Your Way   55
    Your Inner Path   58

Chapter 7
A Brain, A Heart, And Courage   63

    Dorothy   63
    Have You Been Searching... Searching For Something?   64

Chapter 8
The Dot   71

    The Dot   71
    What The Creative Practices Can Do For You   73
    What The Creative Practices Have Done For Me   74

Chapter 9
Squirrel-Itis   79

    Purple-Quilly   79
    Focusing On What You Do Want   82
    You Were Born An Artist   82
    Comparison Is A Terrible Torture!   83

Chapter 10
Breaking Free   89

    Breaking Free   89
    Reframing Negative Self-Talk   92
    Understanding What You Can & Can't Control   93
    How To Focus On The Solution?   95

Chapter 11
It's A Wonderful Life   101

    Angel Clarence   101
    Mastering The Art Of Asking   104

Chapter 12
Meditation In A Strange Place   **111**

    Meditation In A Strange Place   111
    Take A Deep Breath   114
    The Shake It Off Method   117
    Gratitude   119
    Saying Thank You!   120
    The Magic Of Saying "Thank You."   121
    Moving Meditations   123

Chapter 13
The Secret Sauce   **129**

    Alone   129
    Self-criticism is downright hazardous to your health!   132
    Respect Yourself By Speaking Compassionately
    To Yourself   133
    Reflecting and Curiosity   135
    Bring in Your Angel, and ask her to help you!   135
    Focusing On Your Strengths   139
    The Importance Of "Yet"   142

Chapter 14
Finding Funny   **149**

    Humor   149
    You Are What You Put In Or Allow In Your Atmosphere   151

Chapter 15
The Wise Farmer   **159**

    The Wise Farmer   159
    Understanding Expectations   161
    Don't Throw The Baby Out With The Bathwater   161
    Action vs. Acceptance   163
    The Power Of: Or Something Better…   163
    Navigating Expectations   164

Chapter 16
Metamorphosis   **169**
Metamorphosis   169
Transformation   170
Interrupting The Hypnotic State   173

Chapter 17
The Alchemist   **181**
The Alchemist   181
Response-Ability   183
Ways To Become Response-Able   185
Small Steps = Strong Habits   186
Take Action   188

Chapter 18
The Lady In White   **193**
Lady In White   193
Creating Belief   195
How To Communicate With Your Angel   196
Practice Finding Your Angel   196

Chapter 19
ISH   **201**
ISH   201
Using The Creative Practice Part II   203

Chapter 20
Lilly And The Angel   **213**
Lilly & The Angel   213
Writing & Speaking Out Loud   215
Asking Your Angel Practice   219
What Will You Ask Of Your Angel?   223
The Power & Harmony Of Writing   224
Writing   225
Angel Writing   226

Chapter 21
The Angel Doll   235
    The Angel Doll   235

Chapter 22
Creativity Like A Dance   245
    Creativity — Like A Dance   245
    Creating An Inspiration Wall   248

Chapter 23
Dear Art Angel   255
    Art Journaling Is An Anything-Goes Process   255
    Angel Art Journaling   258

Chapter 24
When You Wish Upon A Star   267
    When You Wish Upon A Star   267
    Transformational Asking!   268
    Repetition, Repetition, Repetition…   272
    What if I'm sick?   272

Chapter 25
Remember To Remember   281
    Remember To Remember   281
    Ways To Create An Anchor   285

Chapter 26
Stone Soup   291
    Stone Soup   291
    When The World Changes   293
    Internet Isolation   294
    The Transformative Power Of Community   297

"Everybody has a creative potential and from the moment you can express this creative potential, you can start changing the world." — **Paulo Coelho**

"You use a glass mirror to see your face. You use works of art to see your soul." — **George Bernard Shaw**

"Creativity is inventing, experimenting, growing, taking risks, breaking rules, making mistakes, and having fun." — **Mary Lou Cook**

"Every human is an artist. The dream of your life is to make beautiful art." — **Don Miguel Ruiz**

You can't use up creativity. The more you use, the more you have.

— *Maya Angelou*

"A creative life is an amplifed life. It's a bigger life, a happier life, an expanded life, and a hell of a lot more interesting life. Living in this manner-continually and subbornly bringing forth the jewels that are hidden within you - is a fine art, in and of itself."
— **Elizabeth Gilbert**

"I'm not very creative" doesn't work. There's no such thing as creative people and non-creative people. There are only people who use their creativity and people who don't. Unused creativity isn't benign. It lives within us until it's expressed, neglected to death, or suffocated by resentment and fear." — **Brené Brown**

"We cannot direct the wind, but we can adjust the sails."
— **Dolly Parton**

"The most important words you will ever hear in your entire life are the words you say to yourself."
— **Marisa Peer**

Just keep coming home to yourself, you are the one who you've been waiting for." —**Byron Katie**

"No matter what your age or your life path, whether making art is your career or your hobby or your dream, it is not too late or too egotistical or too selfish or too silly to work on your creativity."— **Julia Cameron**

"A community is a group of people who agree to grow together. The more people you inspire, the more people will inspire you." — **Simon Sinek**

I saw the angel in the marble and carved until I set him free.

— *Michelangelo*

Chapter 1
The Origins Of Angels

The Gifts And Messages From Your Angel

What role do Angels play in my life?

Angels Are Always Present

The idea of this Angel Book came to me and helped me through my darkest hours in 2020. I had been thinking about Angels and doing some research on how they are here to help us. Some of these things resonated with me, especially the idea that **Angels are always present.**

Do you feel alone? As if there is no one to ask for the emotional help and support you need? I'm here to tell you that you are not alone; you are never alone! **Your Angel is here to support you, and in this book, you will learn how to ask for and receive the help you have been looking for all this time!**

The Finding YOUR Angel book that you hold in your hands is a gift that I want to give to you. I believe in the powers of a personal Angel that you can communicate with during those moments when you seek support and assistance in navigating the turbulent waves of life.

This desire and need for such support is not modern or new. It comes to this world from the long corridors of human history.

For thousands of years, numerous cultures incorporated, interpreted, and re-defined the idea of Angels.

So, you stand on the spiritual shoulders of thousands of years of belief in these "messengers" that have the power to communicate and transform your life.

> **Angels by trade are messengers and they are as real as you want them to be. Calling upon them can bring comfort, healing, and courage.**

Many would say an Angel is God's Messenger. If you have ever struggled with religion or the name, God, let's just stick with Messenger… shall we?

And these Messengers love to do their job!

> **Your Angel, however, the one of love and messages, is here to help YOU in any area of your life!**

Angels are a big, bright topic, one that thrills me and gives me purpose. They create a childlike sense of wonder and belief—no matter how troubling the world may seem. When I wake up each day, look out the window at mostly sunny skies, and focus on what makes me feel good, I can see that the world is still a very, very good place in many, many ways.

Throughout history there are stories of these messengers; some have halos, and some have wings. You can see them portrayed as Cupid, helpers, or spirits who intervene when you need them most. We also see people on their knees asking them for help and guidance. They are considered Angelic Beings, sometimes with wings that are thick like a bird and other times translucent like butterfly wings, and still others… iridescent as if not from this world at all.

> **An Angel is a Messenger. They always have a message for you, all you have to do is ASK.**

The Gifts of Angels

Angels transcend boundaries, offering comfort, healing, courage, and guidance. This book serves as a gift and a guide to help you connect with Your Personal Angel to access the support and profound impact Your Angel can have on your life. As we begin this journey together, let us remember Michelangelo's words, "I saw the angel in the marble and carved until I set him free." Like the sculptor, **you too have the power to unveil the Angel within yourself, to connect with their guidance, and to experience the transformative power of their messages.** By opening your heart and mind, by asking and receiving, you unlock the immense potential and peace that lives within you.

As you move through these chapters, remember that you can bring Your Angel with you into the deepest darkest depth, and to your highest enlightened height. They are ever-present, waiting for you to call upon them. Embrace the wonders that unfold as you awaken to Your Angel in your life.

> *"There is a truth deep down inside of you that has been waiting for you to discover it, and that truth is this: you deserve all good things life has to offer."* — Rhonda Byrne

In this first chapter, you are presented with the notion that Angels are messengers and they are always present. They are inviting you to seek comfort from them and allow their presence and guidance to lead you toward a life filled with purpose, joy, and endless possibilities. Remember Tesla's genius that in the pursuit of unlocking the secrets of the universe, you must think in terms of energy, frequency, and vibration, for Angels are the embodiment of these divine forces, ready to dance alongside you on your amazing journey of self-enrichment, fulfillment, and transformation.

At the end of each chapter, you will find a **What If…** question. This is something to ask yourself based on the insights from each chapter.

You will also see a **Dear Angel** sentence. These are examples of ways that you can start to write and speak to Your Angel.

Lastly, you will find **Creative Practice** prompts which are ways to engage in writing and/or doodling to reinforce the insights you receive from each chapter. When you make notes, highlight, write, draw, or doodle, the learning becomes somatic and more ingrained in you. **Take a little time at the end of each chapter to utilize the space provided in this book or start up a journal or sketchbook to capture your thoughts and ideas about Your Angel and the Creative Practices.**

What if... I believe that I truly have my own Personal Angel, just waiting to help and guide me? What would I ask of My Angel?

Dear Guardian Angel, I feel scared and anxious about the ways of the world these days. Please help comfort and reassure me that things will be okay. Please send me messages that will guide me to see more of the beauty in the world and of the goodness in people. Thank you!

Angel Doodle:

- Imagine receiving a message from Your Angel.
- Think about what you'd want Your Angel to say or share with you.
- Write or doodle about this envisioned communication.

Go ahead, jump in! Engage in these Creative Practices, as they will assist you in processing and retaining the information at a much deeper level.

In the next chapter, let's discover the power of belief...

The strongest factor for success is self-esteem: Believing you can do it, believing you deserve it, believing you will get it.

— *John Assaraf*

Chapter 2
Belief Like A Feather

Becoming Solution Oriented

Why? Why should I believe in Angels?

Dumbo

In the beloved Disney story of "Dumbo," a tiny elephant with enormous ears discovers the magic of self-belief and the transformative power of a simple feather. Dumbo, initially lacking confidence, learns that holding a feather gives him the ability to fly. Little does he realize that the feather itself holds no real power—it is merely a symbol of his own belief in himself. As Dumbo emerges into breathtaking flights, captivating audiences with his aerial mastery, he soon realizes **that the feather was never the source of his ability to soar; it was his inner strength and newfound self-confidence that allowed him to achieve the impossible.**

The feather serves as a reminder that true magic lies within you, waiting to be unlocked through self-belief and embracing your unique qualities.

There are magical worlds that Walt Disney and many other animators and fiction writers have created. Walt Disney wanted to get into the hearts of the child-like mind. I dare ask - if you watch any of his movies, do they take you somewhere? Do they ask you to enter a world that if we analyze it seems unreal? But do you also love to get lost in them? Or, have you grown weary of such fairy tales? And, you just don't want to indulge in that child-like behavior or belief system again?

JK Rowling also created a magical world with Harry Potter! Her work allowed millions if not billions to believe! An entire empire has been built upon an idea, a feeling, a download from her imagination which became an entire universe.

I like to think that it was an Angel who shared these stories with JK Rowling. An Angel who knew what she was capable of doing. An Angel who chose her to bring to the world amazing stories and adventures. Her work and her belief in her work created a new world of communities, and connected families and friends. What she has created is truly… magical!

So... What Are Angels?

I propose that Angels are whatever you want and need them to be. In these chapters, I suggest that they are messengers with whom YOU can communicate with and invite into your life.

Bring in Your Angel, and make him or her the very best friend that you have always dreamed of and wanted. One that listens to you, one that makes you feel heard and loved, one that truly wants the very best life for you.

 "You always get what you unconsciously believe and expect. You want to become aware of your thoughts, you want to choose your thoughts carefully and you want to have fun with this, because you are the masterpiece of your own life. You are the Michelangelo of your own life. The David that you are sculpting is you. And you do it with your thoughts." — Dr. Joe Vitale

Why Believe?

Believing will increase your passion for life. When you believe in something you DO want, it can assist you in being inspired to move towards it. Believing in something you DO want can help you become more confident in figuring out how to attain it. Believing helps you move through your life more confidently and with more joy, happiness, and fulfillment. **The power of your belief controls your life.**

"All behavior is driven by belief, so before we address how to learn, we must first address the underlying beliefs we hold about what is possible." — Jim Kwik

What is Essential to Believe?

- Believe in Your Angel, it's the number one way to bring Your Angel into your life.

- Believe the answer is available for you by learning to ask for what you want.

- Believe that you can do it, ask for what you want, and then take action towards it.

- Believe you deserve it, Your Angel will provide!

- Let go of what others think and believe in what YOU want!

When asking of Your Angel, remember not to ask for someone else or something else to change, but ASK instead of how YOU can change to meet the situation. Ask for clarity, ask for strength, ask for patience, ask for the SOLUTION.

Remember this…

- When you focus on the problem,
  --- > more problems arise.
- When you focus on the Solution,
  --- > more Solutions will become clear and available to you.

Let this become your new habit and your life will shift in the most wonderful of ways.

> Have you ever thought; whilst looking all this time for the magic in the world, it's been inside you all along? No matter how far you travel, how wide you spread your wings and learn to fly if you have no idea what treasures hide within you you'll be searching your entire life.
>
> — *Nikki Rowe*

This chapter emphasizes the power of belief and explores the significance of Your Angel's presence in your life. It references stories like "Dumbo" and the magical world of Harry Potter to illustrate the transformative nature of belief. This chapter encourages you to believe in your own Personal Angel and to embrace the knowing that you can communicate with and bring Your Angel into your everyday life. It highlights the importance of belief in creating what you want and guides you to shift your focus toward finding solutions. This chapter urges you to know that the source of your strength (the feather) has always been within you and to be open to that knowing and believing.

What if... just for today, I allowed myself to truly embrace the power of believing in My Angel?

Dear Angel of Belief, let me believe in you today. Let me know that you are here with me and to be open to the messages you share with me. Let me see this in the relationships I have, in the work I do, and in the creativity that bubbles up within me. Thank You!

Creative Practice

Belief Doodle :

- ❤ Write about what Your Angel wants you to believe.

- ❤ Draw, write, or doodle about signs and messages that might have come from Your Angel.

- ❤ Include items you've found such as coins, feathers, numerical sequences such as 11:11, 2:22, 5:55 on a clock, or meaningful coincidences or serendipities that made you stop and wonder…

- ❤ Write these and keep them in mind for the day. You just might be amazed at what turns up for you next!

Coming up next, you'll discover the exact formula you need to call upon Your Angel at any time…

Ask for what you want. Believe that you deserve it, and then allow Life to give it to you.

— **Louise Hay**

Chapter 3
I Think I Can

Using Repetition To Get What You Want

What is the formula for calling on My Angel?

The Little Engine That Could

Once upon a time, there was a Little Blue Engine that faced a big problem. There was a train that needed help, but none of the bigger engines wanted to lend a hand. They all had their reasons and said they couldn't do it. However, the little blue engine, though lacking confidence at first, decided to step up and give it a try.

With a positive attitude and self-belief, the little engine started its journey. It repeated to itself, "I think I can, I think I can, I think I can." Despite the steep hill and the heavy rain, the engine didn't give up. It pushed forward with determination, saying, "I know I can, I know I can, I know I can." And guess what? After a lot of hard work, the little engine made it to the top of the hill, **showing everyone that belief in oneself and**

perseverance can overcome any obstacles. And the Little Blue Engine reflected with… "I thought I could, I thought I could, I thought I could."

So, the story of "The Little Engine That Could" by Watty Piper teaches you the importance of a positive mindset, self-belief, and resilience. It demonstrates that with determination and self-belief, you can overcome challenges and achieve great things.

Your Angel & Repetition

Your Angel has her own battle scars, but it doesn't prevent her from wanting the best for you. In fact, it helps her empathize even more with what you're going through. Her love for you is pure, and it always has been.

> **It's essential to remember that you need to Ask and Take Action.**

Repetition is a fundamental principle of learning. As children, you had to recite your A B C's daily. Every skill you acquired, from walking and talking to eating, reading, and writing, was learned through repetition. It worked for you as a child, so why do you now believe that anything new you want to do should come easily without practice or repetition?

> **Repetition is the key to learning, and you know this because of where and who you are today. Whether it's forming good habits or bad habits, everything you do or don't want is a result of repetition.**

Repetition helps you form new habits. **By repeating a behavior over and over, it becomes automatic, making it easier for you to stick to the new habit or routine.** Even giving up the notion that you need to do things perfectly the first time requires repetition. It takes time and practice.

> *"Repetition is the mother of learning, the father of action, which makes it the architect of accomplishment."* — Zig Ziglar

The quote "anything you want is on the other side of practice" by Jack Canfield, serves as a powerful reminder that achieving anything worthwhile requires effort and persistence. It doesn't have to be hard; you just need to practice and be consistent.

Repetition is the number one skill for development and for achieving anything you set out to accomplish. Embracing repetition requires self-care, practice, and patience. Over time, repetition helps you be more present and forms the automatic habits you desire.

Repetition enhances creativity, as your mind naturally explores new ideas through repetition. Drawing shapes and patterns in repetition is a fantastic exercise that can generate new variations and offer a calming and meditative experience.

> **Repetition is an essential habit for learning and skill development, enabling you to create and explore. You need repetition, practice, play, and variety to avoid getting stuck in a rut or becoming overly rigid in your thinking and behavior.**

Repetition creates muscle memory, allowing you to remember specific pieces of music, writings, dance moves, and all artistic expressions.

What Do I Call My Angel?

"What's in a name? That which we call a rose by any other name would smell just as sweet."
— William Shakespeare - Romeo and Juliet

The essence of Your Angel goes beyond the name or label you give them. This is Your Angel. Name her whatever you like.

She is here in her perfect imperfections, like life, like love, like you, like me.

She is here in her perfect imperfections, like life, like love, like you, like me.

Here Is The Secret To Calling In Your Angel…

In your times of need, pain, impatience, anger, rage, frustration, hurt, disbelief, or disappointment
—CALL OUT LOUD TO YOUR ANGEL.

"Clarity comes from action, not thought."
— Marie Forleo

Some Names You Can Call Your Angel

- Angel
- My Angel
- Archangel
- Guardian Angel
- Messenger
- The Angel of… (this could be the Angel of Healing, Angel of Patience, Angel of Messages, etc…)

Name Her Whatever You Like. It can be your favorite name, the name of someone who inspires you, the name of a past loved one, or simply... Angel.

You get to choose how to address Your Angel. Approach Your Angel with respect, gratitude, and openness to receive her guidance, messages, and healing.

Your Angel can be male or female, young or old, playful or serious—a mother, a teacher, like a butterfly, or anything you can imagine.

"We simply need to believe in the power that's within us and use it." — Benjamin Hoff
- The Tao of Pooh

What Is The Formula For Calling On Your Angel?

In your time of need, pain, impatience, anger, rage, frustration, or disappointment, just call OUT LOUD to Your Angel.

- Call her by NAME.
- ASK her to RELEASE you from any discomfort or dis-ease.
- Say OUT LOUD what you DO want.
- Ask for Clarity.
- Ask for the Solution.
- Ask and Believe in Your Angel!
- Take Action!

Take whatever action is necessary to do your part, even if it's just asking yourself to take a step in the direction of the solution. If that's not the case and it's something you need to let go of, ask Your Angel to help you let go and shift your focus elsewhere for a time.

This formula has worked wonders for me and all who use it consistently. It has helped me ASK for the SOLUTION and step out of the hopelessness and harmful negative self-talk that had plagued me for most of my life.

Thank You, Thank You, Thank You!

Your Angel doesn't expect anything in return, but I love to reflect back and notice when the bad feeling has left, then say her name out loud again and say... **"Thank you, thank you, thank you!"** In my mind, they appreciate this, just as anyone would appreciate a 'Thank You' after they have helped someone.

> *"The eight laws of learning are explanation, demonstration, imitation, repetition, repetition, repetition, repetition, repetition."*
> *— John Wooden*

This chapter explores the power of belief and the magical success that comes with using repetition to get what you want. The story "The Little Engine That Could" is used to emphasize the importance of a positive mindset and perseverance. This chapter encourages you to recite your beliefs, choose a name for Your Angel, and call on Your Angel out loud to ask for what you want and to seek clarity. It emphasizes the significance of repetition in learning and embracing new skills while also engaging in Creative Practices.

What if... I called upon My Angel by name, expressing my desires out loud, and asking for clarity, guidance, and healing?

Dear Angel of Peace, let me call upon you today, asking out loud for what it is I DO want and I ask you to remove any suffering I don't need. Please replace those hard feelings with lightness and ease, hope and joy, wonder and curiosity! Thank you, thank you, thank you!

Creative Practice

Finding Your Angel Doodle:

- Write out some of the possible names of Your Angel or simply write "Angel."

- Begin to doodle around the letters and get curious about what will happen, let it happen, let go, and see where the doodling takes you.

Ahead, you'll understand how to connect with Your Personal Angel to support and guide you on your journey…

Success is built on small victories and incremental progress. The all-or-nothing mindset only hinders your journey.

— *Simon Sinek*

Chapter 4
Finding The Middle Ground

Releasing the All-Or-Nothing Mindset

How can I become more flexible in my mind?

Does It Have To Be All-Or-Nothing?

During a discussion about the all-or-nothing mindset with a hypnotherapy client of mine, she had an epiphany! She used to believe that she had to strictly adhere to things as they were presented—no deviations, no flexibility. It was the classic all-or-nothing mindset.

Starting a new diet? It had to be all-or-nothing.

Beginning a new program? Clear the calendar and jump all in or let it sit there forever. Discovering a new art method? Get all the supplies or don't bother trying.

> **But after these exhausting attempts and the feelings of failure surrounding them, she realized that her true nature is to extract those precious nuggets that truly resonate with her, experiment with them, and then let go of the rest or revisit them at a later time.**

Life doesn't have to be black-or-white, all-or-nothing. There's a value scale and color wheel of options in between.

So many people fall into the all-or-nothing trap, believing that they must adhere to a program entirely or not at all. However, it's clear to witness that this often leads to feelings of personal failure.

The truth is every book is authored by and for the writer. While we hope to share and assist you based on our experiences, let's face it— **we are all ohhhhh soooooooo human.**

No one is perfect. Seriously, no one! And speaking of perfection, what is that anyway? Who sets the standards for perfect or normal?

In my search for perfect people, I've come to realize they don't exist. But my mind still thinks they might, and the day I find that perfect person will probably be the same day I find a Unicorn… It could happen… it just hasn't happened… yet!

I've encountered artists who are both happy and miserable, successful business people who experience both joy and despair and individuals of various body types with different levels of health.

FINDING THE MIDDLE GROUND

What matters most is that **you** understand who **YOU** are and **discover what works for you.**

Your life is uniquely yours, your processes are distinct, and your outlook is personal. While there may be areas of common ground, everyone is traveling on their own bumpy and windy road.

You may have encountered numerous friendships, relationships, and work interactions. Although you may resonate more with certain people, no one is exactly like you, and you are not exactly like anyone else. With this understanding, **you are encouraged to take from this book what truly works for you.** You are not obligated to adopt everything or even a portion of this book. **Embrace only what resonates with your true authentic self.**

Finding yourself is something many of us try to do. Looking for what you are good at or what you think you *"should"* focus on. Most people in your life will probably have a suggestion for you as to what to do and what not to do… and some people just have the need to reinvent the wheel for themselves.

Have you ever met someone so talented, like a pianist, but the person just isn't interested in making a career out of it? You may think to yourself, "Gosh, if I had their talent, I would play the piano all day long." There are so many stories of people like this, where someone is amazing at something or naturally talented, and everyone around them thinks that this is their path, the way they *"should"* go. But they just are not passionate about it. It could be a true lackluster for it, or it could be all the pressure from other people, and they rebel.

> *"My father could have been a great comedian but he didn't believe that that was possible for him, and so he made a conservative choice. Instead, he got a safe job as an accountant and when I was 12 years old he was let go from that safe job, and our family had to do whatever we could to survive. I learned many great lessons from my father. Not the least of which was that: You can fail at what you don't want. So, you might as well take a chance on doing what you love."*
> — *Jim Carrey*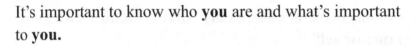

It's important to know who **you** are and what's important to **you.**

It's great to encourage others with talents you believe they have, but ultimately, **it's their own life to create their own journey.**

Approach this book and everything in your life in a way that you understand and that feels appropriate to you and your values. Yes, it's important to grow and sometimes growth is uncomfortable.

> **However, by embracing the parts that genuinely speak to you, they will naturally become a part of your journey and will be worth some of the "learning and practicing something new discomfort" of making these things new and consistent habits for you.**

Changing The All-Or-Nothing Mindset

The all-or-nothing mindset can stem from a variety of sources and experiences. Here are a few possible factors that can contribute to the all-or-nothing mindset and how to begin shifting it:

- **PERFECTIONISM:** The desire for perfection and the fear of making mistakes can lead to an all-or-nothing mindset. Perfectionists often believe that if they can't do something perfectly, it's just not worth doing at all.

  - **Instead, let's practice embracing PROGRESS over PERFECTION.** See if you can shift your focus from that unattainable perfection to the little steps toward your progress. Celebrate every step forward, no matter how small, and acknowledge that setbacks are just stepping stones to success, they are natural and sometimes even necessary.

- **FEAR OF FAILURE:** Some people fear failure so much that they adopt an all-or-nothing mindset. They believe that if they can't achieve complete success, it's better not to try at all to avoid the possibility of failure.

  - **Rather, Redefine Your Own Success.** Free yourself to define success based on your values, your passions, and your personal journey. Celebrate all of your achievements no matter how big or small they may be. Remind yourself of what makes you feel happy, fulfilled, driven, and passionate.

Here are several quotes from some well-known people leaving you clues on how 'failure' will actually lead to success.

> *"We need to accept that we won't always make the right decisions, that we'll screw up royally sometimes – understanding that failure is not the opposite of success, it's part of success."*
> *— Arianna Huffington*

> *"Failure is another stepping stone to greatness."*
> *— Oprah Winfrey*

> *"Our greatest glory is not in never failing, but in rising every time we fail." — Confucius*

> *"Those who dare to fail miserably can achieve greatly." — John F. Kennedy*

Is this being driven home? If not… here are a few more…

> *"You build on failure. You use it as a stepping stone." — Johnny Cash*

Trust me, I know about the fear of failure. In writing this book, I have to Ask My Angel to help me keep my but in the chair writing and editing without knowing if it will be any good at all. I have to finish this book, I have to risk its failure to be able to taste its success!

"Failure is success in progress."
— *Albert Einstein*

"I've missed more than 9000 shots in my career. I've lost almost 300 games. 26 times, I've been trusted to take the game-winning shot and missed. I've failed over and over and over again in my life. And that is why I succeed."
— *Michael Jordan*

"Failure happens all the time. it happens every day in practice. What makes you better is how you react to it." — *Mia Hamm*

…and to drive this home just a bit more, I'll end with these two quotes…

 "I have not failed. I have found 10,000 ways that don't work." — *Thomas Edison*

"Courage allows the successful woman to fail and learn powerful lessons from the failure. So that in the end, she didn't fail at all."
— *Maya Angelou*

→ **BLACK & WHITE THINKING:** People with a tendency for black-and-white thinking see the world in extremes and struggle to find a middle ground. They view situations as either all good or all bad, with no room for shades of gray.

- **Alternatively, Embrace The Gray Areas:** Challenge the habit of black-and-white thinking and embrace the nuances and complexities of life. Explore alternative perspectives, realizing that there can be more than one right answer or approach. You can start by asking Your Angel to show you more options or to investigate and research alternative approaches or thought processes about the subject.

→ **SOCIETAL & CULTURAL INFLUENCES:** Societal and cultural pressures can contribute to the all-or-nothing mindset as well. Messages emphasizing the importance of achievement, success, and perfection can lead you to believe that anything less than total success is a failure.

- **Instead, Cultivate Self-Compassion:** Treat yourself with kindness, understanding, and forgiveness. Embrace self-compassion as a guiding light, allowing room for mistakes, imperfections, and the inevitable setbacks that organically come with growth.

→ **PAST EXPERIENCES:** Previous experiences of success or failure can shape the way you approach new challenges. If you have experienced success by giving your all, you may feel that the same level of dedication is necessary in all situations. Similarly, past failures may reinforce the belief that anything less than complete effort is insufficient.

- **Embrace Flexibility:** Life is ever-changing, and adapting to new circumstances is crucial. Cultivate flexibility in your thinking and approach, allowing for creative solutions and resilient navigation of challenges.

> **It's important to assess that the all-or-nothing mindset may not be beneficial in most situations. It can limit personal growth, hinder decision-making, and lead to feelings of frustration and disappointment. Nurturing a more balanced and flexible mindset can help you navigate challenges and find more sustainable approaches to achieving your goals.**

Escaping the clutches of the all-or-nothing mindset requires courage and a willingness to embrace a different perspective. By acknowledging how you may have created the all-or-nothing mindset, and then consciously adopting a more nurturing and flexible mindset, you can break free from its limitations. Embrace progress, seek the beauty in the gray areas, and redefine success on your own terms. With self-compassion and flexibility as your friends, you can travel through life's challenges and savor the journey, your growth, and the fulfillment that awaits you.

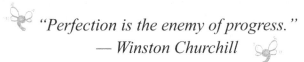

"Perfection is the enemy of progress."
— *Winston Churchill*

After experiencing the transformative power of a Rapid Transformational Therapy (RTT) session in 2017, I knew I had to become a practitioner to help people transform their lives, just as my session had transformed me. My teacher, Marisa Peer, a world-renowned hypnotherapist, employs some extraordinary approaches, and one of her most impactful lessons is: **"To succeed at anything, you have to make the unfamiliar familiar and the familiar unfamiliar."** This means practicing the positive actions and beliefs of things that are currently unfamiliar to you to make them familiar through repetition. So, if you want to break free from all-or-nothing thinking or any other unhelpful pattern, you must shift your focus toward what you do want (the unfamiliar) rather than dwelling on what you don't want (the familiar)."

Life is a curious dance, and sometimes it's about going with the rhythm and flow rather than forcing a rigid structure. Embrace the moments of spontaneity, allow yourself to pause and appreciate the present. Notice where you can find joy in some of the simple pleasures along the way.

> *"Optimist: Someone who figures that taking a step backward after taking a step forward is not a disaster, it's a cha-cha."* — Robert Brault

---

Above all, be kind and compassionate to yourself. This journey is not about perfection or reaching some final destination. It's about embracing your purpose in life and finding lots of little and lovely things to be grateful for and nurtured by.

Small accomplishments pave the road to enrichment in this chapter. Trust yourself and find the rhythm that works for you. By releasing fear, embracing flexibility, and re-framing the all-or-nothing mindset, you can feel more fulfilled and truly transform your life. Your Angel is by your side, and with focus, repetition, and trust in yourself, you can accomplish anything. Remember, change and fulfillment are within your reach, one little baby step at a time.

You can do anything, but not everything.

— *David Allen*

What if... I let My Angel help me become more flexible by asking for help to find the middle ground?

Dear Angel of Flexibility, please let my mind be flexible enough to understand different personality types and to stay strong and true to the path I know is meant for me. Thank you, thank you, thank you.

Creative Practice

Release Doodle:

- Draw a trash can (or use the one provided).
- Place things, belief systems, and past experiences you want to let go of into the trash can.
- Scribble all over it until it feels gone!

Moving right along, let's dive into the significance of embracing a beginner's mind and what cultivating curiosity can do for your life…

www.NicoleWhiteWellness.com

In the beginner's mind, there are many possibilities, but in the expert's mind, there are few.

— *Shunryu Suzuki*

Chapter 5
Curiosità

Removing The Obstacles

What is the significance of embracing a Beginner's Mind and Cultivating Curiosity?

Obstacle Course

I remember Tony Robbins sharing a story about learning how to drive a race car. His driving instructor advised him to "Focus on where you want to go, not on where you don't want to go."

While on an obstacle course with his instructor, he was set up to go into a spin and had to make his way out of it. He said that he couldn't help but keep his eyes locked on the wall he desperately wanted to avoid (that's the habit). His instructor had to physically push his face to look at the clear road ahead, the direction he actually wanted to go (the solution).

Tony learned a powerful lesson from that experience; If you constantly focus on what you don't want, you end up being drawn toward it. But when you shift your attention to what you do want, you will find yourself naturally moving in the direction you want to go.

> *"Wherever focus goes, energy flows"*
> *— Tony Robbins*

Adopting A Beginner's Mind

> *"Shoshin" is a concept from Zen Buddhism meaning beginner's mind. It refers to having an attitude of openness, eagerness, and lack of preconception when studying a subject, even at an advanced level, just as a beginner would. The term is especially used in the study of Zen Buddhism and Japanese martial arts."*
> *— Wikipedia*

It's crucial to become aware of where you direct your attention. When you catch yourself fixated on what you don't want, it's time to consciously redirect your focus towards what you do want.

> **Your attention is a compass; be mindful of where it points. When it lingers on what you fear, steer it deliberately towards what you desire.**

CURIOSITÀ

So… are you ready? Ready to embrace the concept of "Beginner's Mind" and apply it to your life? Instead of getting caught up in the overwhelming aspects of the problem, begin to focus on what you can do, it can be as simple as Asking Your Angel to help you with the matter at hand.

By shifting your attention towards your desired outcome, you create space for positive change and possibilities to emerge. So, let your gaze be directed towards the open road ahead, where solutions await and a brighter path unfolds.

Beginner's Mind asks you to **Focus** on the things that YOU CAN DO, even if you are just asking for some relief in your emotions toward the solution.

> **As you move through this book, you will notice many areas of repetition. When you find yourself thinking, "I know this already" or "I've heard this before," I encourage you to pause… and embrace curiosity. Instead of dismissing it as repetitive, explore what messages it holds for you in this unique instance.**

See if you can be open to the chance that a fresh perspective or deeper understanding awaits, ready to reveal itself when approached with an open mind. So, begin this journey with a receptive spirit, and let the echoes of repetition guide you towards newfound insights.

"Sell your cleverness and buy bewilderment." — Rumi

I Wonder...

Let's introduce a game called **"I Wonder"** that you can play to cultivate your beginner's mind and start investing in curiosity instead of fixed thinking:

"I Wonder" is a playful and contemplative activity inspired by the concept of "shoshin" or beginner's mind. It involves cultivating a sense of curiosity, openness, and non-judgment towards yourself and the world around you.

To play the game, intentionally adopt a beginner's mindset, letting go of any preconceived notions or biases. Approach situations, challenges, or problems with a genuine sense of wonder and curiosity, as if encountering them for the very first time.

When faced with a problem, pause… and ask yourself, "I wonder..." followed by a question that opens up new possibilities. For example, "I wonder what would happen if I approached this differently?" or "I wonder what creative solutions I haven't considered yet?"

As you ask these open-ended "I wonder" questions, you explore new ideas and perspectives, breaking free from habitual thinking and encouraging creativity, curiosity, and innovation.

The game nurtures self-inquiry and curiosity, fostering personal growth and understanding. By embracing the unknown, you cultivate receptivity and discovery.

Start Small:

Think about a small problem or issue in your life. Begin with something simple, such as a minor annoyance or a task you are procrastinating on. Choose something manageable that doesn't feel overwhelming. Once you learn this process, it will be easier to apply it to bigger issues in your life.

EXAMPLE:

- My roommate never washes their dishes, and it frustrates me.
- It creates a messy and unpleasant environment in the kitchen.
- I end up washing their dishes, which feels unfair.
- We've had discussions about this issue before, but it doesn't seem to change anything.

Cross Out Anything That Is Out Of Your Control:

- ~~My roommate never washes their dishes~~ (out of your control).
- ~~We've had discussions about this issue, but it doesn't seem to change~~ (out of your control).

Use "I wonder" statements to shift your perspective and incorporate asking for help:

- I wonder what would happen if I approached this issue with empathy and tried to understand my roommate's perspective on cleanliness?

- ? I wonder how it would feel to address the problem calmly and assertively, without getting angry or frustrated?

- ? I wonder if there are any alternative solutions to keeping the kitchen clean that we haven't explored yet?

- ? I wonder how our communication and relationship would improve if I focused on finding common ground and compromise?

Add The Aspect Of Asking For Help From Your Angel:

> **Something truly amazing happens when you ask Your Angel a Question! Your Angel WANTS to answer you!**

- ? **I wonder** what would happen if I asked My Angel for guidance and assistance in finding a resolution to this issue?

- ? **I wonder** how my perspective would shift if I actively sought support from My Angel in dealing with this situation?

- ? **I wonder** what would happen if, just for today, every time this problem arises, I shift my focus from the old story and the problem's details and instead ask aloud, "What is the solution here?"

- ? **I wonder** how things would change if I approached this situation with a beginner's mind, free from assumptions or fixed beliefs?

- **?** **I wonder** what new insights and possibilities I could discover by releasing my assumptions and approaching this issue with a sense of curiosity and openness?

- **?** **I wonder** how my interactions with others would improve if I genuinely listened to them with an open mind, letting go of my opinions and judgments?

- **?** **I wonder** what creative solutions I might uncover if I allowed myself to explore this challenge with a fresh perspective, as if encountering it for the first time?

Open Up To Embrace Curiosity:

As you ask these "I Wonder" questions, allow yourself to embrace curiosity and openness. Observe your belief patterns and begin to approach them with wonder and a beginner's mind.

Explore The Possibilities:

While asking these questions, take some time to reflect on what has surfaced for you and identify small ways to shift your perspective. Notice shifts in your thinking, new ideas that come to light, or fresh perspectives that you haven't entertained before.

EXAMPLE:
Overcoming Procrastination:

- **?** **I wonder** what would happen if I approached my tasks with a sense of excitement and curiosity?

- **?** **I wonder** how it would feel to complete my tasks with a deep sense of satisfaction and accomplishment?

? **I wonder** what new perspectives could emerge if I break my tasks into smaller, more manageable steps?

? **I wonder** what creative solutions might arise by incorporating fun and playfulness into my work process?

? **I wonder** what lessons I could learn from understanding the underlying reasons for my procrastination?

Feel free to take out a blank piece of paper, and design it creatively if you like, adding visuals, colors, or additional prompts to enhance your *I Wonder* Experience! The goal is to create a space where you can engage with the "I Wonder" game, reflect on your own questions, and explore the power of curiosity and beginner's mind.

For simplicity, here are the questions again. Pick a minor annoyance, write down each of these prompts, and then complete the sentence on your own:

- I wonder what would happen if...
- I wonder how it would feel to...
- I wonder what new perspectives could emerge from...
- I wonder what creative solutions might arise by...
- I wonder what lessons I could learn from...

CURIOSITÀ

> **Playing the "I Wonder" game regularly cultivates a mindset free from preconceptions. It brings more joy, curiosity, and flexibility to your experiences, enabling you to navigate challenges with creativity and curiosity. The purpose is to embrace exploration, not necessarily find immediate answers.**

By focusing on your desired destination rather than fixating on what you don't want, you steer yourself toward your goals. This shift away from problems and towards solutions is a valuable lesson, just as Tony Robbins learned while driving a race car.

Engage in the "I Wonder" game consistently and enjoy the transformative power of approaching life with a beginner's mind. Embrace the joy of exploration and navigate towards your aspirations.

· ♥ · ♥ · ♥ · ♥ · ♥ ·

Get Curious

I wanted to share one more thing that is near and dear to my heart before we close up this chapter… **Curiosità!**

Curiosità - I love this word! I first encountered it when listening to Brian Johnson reading his *Philosopher's Note* about the book "How to Think Like Leonardo da Vinci: Seven Steps to Genius Every Day" by Michael J. Gelb: and have since intentionally added it to my vocabulary.

I love certain words and the way they play and sound. It's one thing to tell myself to be "curious" about something, it's a whole new grand staircase to say Curiosità - and for it to have that **Umph** behind it.

Curiosità is not just a word, it's a **feeeeeeeeeeling** and **sensaaaaaaaaation**. It takes up all body senses, and for some reason, I also smell fresh ground coffee when I say it! For me, it means getting into that creative groove and a little Angel voice saying "You got this!"

> *"Curiosità" is an Italian word that translates to "curiosity" in English. It refers to the desire to learn, explore, and discover new things. It is often associated with a sense of wonder and inquisitiveness, and it can drive individuals to seek out new knowledge and experiences. In Italian culture, "curiosità" is often seen as a positive trait, as it encourages people to be engaged and interested in the world around them."* — Wikipedia

Concluding this chapter, remember the value and power of a beginner's mind to help you cultivate curiosity into your journey. Let yourself be supported by the wisdom and guidance of Your Angel. By adopting a mindset of openness and Curiosità, you can navigate the ups and downs of life, embracing them as opportunities for growth and learning. Life was not meant to be perfect, but with practice, you gain the ability to successfully sail through troubled waters and emerge

CURIOSITÀ

even stronger. Let the "I Wonder" game encourage you to ask thought-provoking questions, explore new ideas, and discover creative solutions for everyday issues. Embrace curiosity, focus on positive outcomes, and set sail on the adventures of self-discovery and transformation. Remember, your path to fulfillment is paved with wonder and the courage to navigate the uncharted seas of life. Embrace the wisdom of each voyage and invite Your Angel into this adventure with you.

Curiosity and creativity are your unique superpowers. The more you use them, the stronger, more powerful, and more creative and curious you become!

What if... I fully embraced the concept of Curiosità and made a habit of playing the "I Wonder" game whenever a stressful issue arose?

Dear Angel of Curiosity, please sprinkle some extra wonder dust on my problems. Help me unravel their mysterious ways, discover their hidden secrets, and playfully kick them to the curb. I'm ready to dance with the unknown, laugh at the absurd, and embrace the lessons that come my way. Thank you for being my partner in crime-solving! You're the best wing-girl any curiosità soul could ask for. Thank you, thank you, thank you!

Creative Practice

Curiosità Doodling:

- Write or doodle about a captivating journey that sparks Curiosità within you.

- Explore things such as travel, nature, cooking, movement, art, science, or even an imaginary adventure.

- Use your creativity to vividly describe the parts of this journey that ignite wonder and curiosity.

Turning the page to the next chapter, you'll encounter the inner compass that can steer you toward your genuine life path and the purposes that resonate most deeply with you…

There is a voice inside of you
That whispers all day long,
'I feel this is right for me,
I know that this is wrong.'
No teacher, preacher,
 parent, friend or
Wise man can decide
What's right for you-just
Listen to The Voice that
speaks inside.

— *The Voice by
Shel Silverstein*

Chapter 6

There Is A Voice Inside Of You

Finding Your Way

Where is the voice within me that can guide me to my true path & purpose in life?

Finding Your Way

> **The way to your path, your true self, and your true purpose in this life is to listen.**

To listen to yourself.

To listen to that inner voice that holds a dream, your dream could encompass anything: flying a plane, writing a book, creating artwork, becoming an athlete, a dancer, a singer, an engineer, a photographer, a cook, a garden designer, or embracing a simple life with a van and the freedom to travel and explore. The possibilities are infinite, and it is within you to pursue and achieve your deepest desires in this life.

To journey towards your true path, your authentic self, and your purpose in this life, it is essential to learn the art of listening. **Listening, not to the noise of the outside world, but to the whispers of your own heart and soul.** Within those whispers are the dreams you held near and dear when you were younger, somewhere between the ages of 7 and 14.

Recall the moments when your imagination soared, and your young spirit danced with possibility. **Remember the dreams that ignited a fire within you, the dreams that painted vibrant pictures in your mind and filled your heart with excitement.** Close your eyes and let the memories wash over you.

Perhaps you experienced a live band and felt the music coursing through your veins, making you dream of becoming a musician. Maybe you even dared to pick up an instrument and explore the melodies that resonated within you.

Or maybe, as you sat in a restaurant, savoring a beautifully presented and delectable meal, you were captivated by the magic of culinary creation. In that moment, you dreamt of becoming a chef, envisioning yourself crafting exquisite dishes that would delight and nourish others.

There might have been a time when you stumbled upon an art gallery, your eyes widening at the colors and creativities on display. That spark of inspiration ignited within you, urging you to pick up a paintbrush and explore your own artistic expressions.

Perhaps, in a moment of stillness by a serene riverbank, you caught a glimpse of a peaceful monk, radiating tranquility and contentment. Their simplicity and inner peace spoke to your soul, igniting a desire within you to seek a life of quiet and spiritual fulfillment.

Now, take a moment to reflect and write down some of those childhood dreams you held close to your heart. Allow them to bubble up to the surface, capturing them on paper as a testament to the pure aspirations of your younger self. **These dreams may hold the keys to your true calling, guiding you back to your authentic path.**

> *"Anybody with artistic ambitions is always trying to reconnect with the way they saw things as a child."* — Tim Burton

Remember, those dreams were not random whispers. They were the echoes of your true essence—the essence that knew what brought you joy and fulfillment before the world had its say. By acknowledging and honoring these childhood dreams, you open yourself up to a deeper understanding of who you are and what truly matters to you.

While it's important to release the grips of the past, including traumas and regrets, it's equally vital to explore certain moments in time to gain valuable insights. This exploration will enable you to transform your past.

In my work with Hypnotherapy clients, I guide them to connect and reshape their connection with their past. By peeking back into those memories, they can extract the desired knowledge and effectively upgrade the impact of those past experiences. This is very much like re-parenting yourself so that you can elevate your inner child to now be able to experience what you want, instead of what may have deterred you back then.

Your Inner Path

Your inner path is always present. It's that little voice inside that will speak up… if you listen. Your inner path holds ideas that, if followed, will bring profound meaning into your life.

This book encourages any Creative Practice to help you rediscover your true north, your path, giving yourself permission to listen and be guided by your inner compass.

If you are willing to go within, to ask the questions, to write down or be in silence and listen for your answers… then you will be amazed and delighted by how you can navigate through your life's experiences.

> **Everything is within you. You exist within the universe, and the universe exists within you. Just as you are An Angel, you have An Angel within you, and Your Angel is with you at all times.**

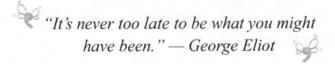

"It's never too late to be what you might have been." — George Eliot

This chapter's emphasis is on listening to your inner voice. Listen to those old childhood dreams and heart whispers that can connect you to your authentic self. Reflect on moments of imagination and aspiration from your past and recognize that these dreams hold the key to your genuine desires. Your past can provide valuable insights and set the stage for future discussions on transforming old experiences. This chapter concludes by highlighting that your inner path holds profound ideas for bringing more meaning and purpose into your life, urging you to embrace and explore your Creative Practice of choice.

Follow your Path
Let yourself Play,
See what Creativity
Guides your WAY !

What if... I allowed myself to dream and write down my true heart's desires?

Dear Angel of Inner Guidance, please help me find my path, my purpose, my north star, my compass rose... Thank you, thank you, thank you.

Creative Practice

North Star Doodles:

- ♥ Doodle a winding path with a North Star as your guiding light.

- ♥ Along the path, write or doodle your heartfelt wishes aligned with the North Star.

- ♥ If you have multiple North Stars, acknowledge all of them.

- ♥ Write and/or doodle about each guiding light.

- ♥ Additionally, you can draw a visual map of your desires, whatever that looks like for you.

In the next chapter, let's uncover what will help you open up and break through any barriers in your life…

Who looks outside, dreams; who looks inside, awakens.

— Carl Jung

Chapter 7

A Brain, A Heart, And Courage

Looking Within

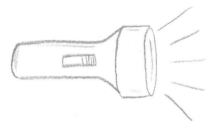

**What will help me open up and break through
the barriers in my life?**

Dorothy

Dorothy goes on a journey along the yellow brick road, hoping to find a way home. Throughout her adventure, she encounters various challenges and meets others who also seek something they believe is outside of themselves… a brain, a heart, and courage.

"The Wizard of Oz" serves as a metaphor for your inner journey of self-discovery and realizing that the things you seek are often already within you. I am referring specifically to the scene where Dorothy discovers that the power to go home was within her all along. **It is through her own strength, resilience, and love for her friends that she overcomes obstacles and eventually finds her way back home to Kansas.**

Have You Been Searching... Searching For Something?

That something that you think will help you open up and break through any barriers created in your life so far? They could have been created by circumstances, by family, by work, or what may seem like accidents.

Have you read books that tell you how to live your life? What time to get up in the morning, what to think during the day, what to eat, how to sleep, how much to work, and so on? Have you read self-help or success books that leave you feeling worse than when you started?

Do you follow people online who seem to have a level of happiness and success that you dream about, only to feel worse or question what you are doing wrong, berating yourself thinking that you can't achieve the same level of success?

Perhaps their process doesn't work for you. It's important to discover what does work for you.

Among the vastly different people in the world, there's a wide range of interests and behaviors. Some people like to wake up early, while others prefer staying up late. Some enjoy being outgoing, while others are more comfortable being alone. Some people love spicy food, and then some can't handle the heat! People have so many different interests – some love reading books, others enjoy watching TV; some like the beach, while others prefer the mountains. Some crave adventure, while others prefer a steady routine. These differences in what people enjoy and how they act all come together to create the diversity of our shared human experience, reminding us of the uniqueness and variety that exists among us.

Just imagine for a moment if everyone was exactly the same! What a static and boring world it would be, wouldn't it? It's the curious oddities and quirky qualities in each of us that add that special 'je ne sais quoi' spice to life. Embracing differences is what makes your journey so much richer and fascinating. So, savor the beauty in your individuality and toast to a life filled with colorful characters and unique paths!

> **I believe the secret you have been looking for is within you. You get to discover what works for you. What motivates you? What kind of routine or non-routine works for you? What do you want? And most importantly... what are you willing to do for it?**

> *"Today you are You,*
> *That is truer than true.*
> *There is no one alive*
> *Who is Youer than You."*
> — Dr. Seuss

See if you can become inspired by your own individuality, cultivating more self-acceptance, and even curiosity about who you truly are.

You have to go within and find a path that works for you, your path! This is the path that will work for you, and you will work for it.

> **It means that you will engage in the practices to create what it is you want. If you are not willing to do the work for what you think you want, then it's important to ask yourself if you really want it if you are not willing to put in the effort.** ⬅ Read that again.

You can always ask Your Angel for the willingness to do what is necessary to achieve what you desire. Make sure that what you want is something you are willing to work for, to embrace in your life, and something that feels right for you!

I've been on a journey of self-evolving for decades, led by disturbing thoughts and feelings called anxiety and depression. My path has been to find a way to quickly remove these negative thoughts and patterns as soon as I notice them.
I do this by first searching for what I want and then asking for it.

"Insanity is doing the same thing over and over again and expecting a different result."
— *Albert Einstein*

If you find yourself falling into the same negative pattern repeatedly, it's time to examine them and see what can be done differently. Be willing to try new approaches and ask for the solution, seek the solution, and it will become clear. You can ask for anything you want, but you also have to be willing to ask for the courage to take the action that is essential to achieving what you want.

 "Process saves us from the poverty of our intentions." — *Elizabeth King*

The messages of this chapter are meant to explore the idea that awakening comes from looking within yourself instead of seeking outside validation or for others to change. Just like Dorothy in "The Wizard of Oz," who ultimately realizes that the power to go home was within her all along, you are encouraged to trust your intuition and find your own unique path to your purpose. Embracing your individuality, acknowledging your desires, and being willing to take action that is aligned with your authentic self are the key elements to uncovering your true potential and creating a more fulfilled life.

What if... I became inspired by my own individuality, cultivating more self-acceptance, and even curiosity about who I truly am?

Dear Angel of Self-Discovery, please help me figure out what I truly want, and then guide me in taking the necessary steps to accomplish it. Thank you, thank you, thank you.

A BRAIN, A HEART, AND COURAGE

Creative Practice

Illuminated Doodles:

- Replicate a flashlight by drawing, tracing, or finding a picture of one.

- Imagine focusing that flashlight on what you want and draw lines for the beams of light coming out of the flashlight.

- Write or draw into the light beams the thing or things you want to accomplish and feel. Let this visual metaphor brighten your path toward the things that truly matter to you.

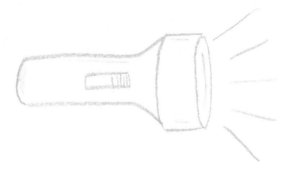

Moving forward, I have an important question for you to ask yourself...

I found I could say things with color and shapes that I couldn't say another way - things I had no words for.

— Georgia O'Keeffe

Chapter 8

The Dot

Creative Practice Part I

What would happen if I believed in myself today?

The Dot

One day, during a break from work, I stumbled upon a charming gift shop. Among the adorable items like a notepad featuring a unicorn with the phrase "be-you-tiful," I noticed a book that immediately caught my attention. Its cover was white, with a large bright orange dot and a young girl holding a giant paintbrush. Assuming it was a children's book, I decided to give it a read. Little did I know that this book would deeply resonate with me. I choked up while reading it and tears welled in my eyes. This is the book that eventually inspired me to create a course called *You CAN Paint!* centered around its message. That book is called "The Dot" by Peter H. Reynolds.

"The Dot" may be found in the children's section, but don't be fooled - it's a hidden gem for adults seeking creative inspiration.

This book tells the story of a young girl named Vashti who believes she can't draw. When her art teacher encourages her to just make a mark on a piece of paper, Vashti reluctantly stabs the paper and draws a simple dot. Her teacher sees potential in that dot and asks Vashti to sign it. The next morning she saw her dot framed above her teacher's desk in "swirly gold."

Inspired, Vashti becomes more confident in her abilities and starts exploring different ways to create art using dots. Eventually, she showcases her dot-inspired artwork at an art exhibition, proving that even a simple dot can be the start of something amazing. **"The Dot" highlights the importance of starting small, which helps you quickly overcome self-doubt.** The young girl believed she couldn't draw, but by taking that first step of making a dot, she discovered her own unlimited creative potential. The book also emphasizes the role of encouragement and mentorship in the creative practices, as well as the idea that creativity knows no bounds and can be expressed in various ways.

> **Through and through this book encourages you to jump in, let go of the all-or-nothing mentality, embrace a beginner's mind, and make your mark. Freeing yourself to get started or continue deeper with your creative journey.**

Overall, "The Dot" serves as a reminder that creativity begins with taking that first courageous step, and it encourages you to embrace your own creative journey, no matter how small or how simple it may start… like a dot.

What The Creative Practices Can Do For You

Many people have incredible stories of experiencing profound healing and personal transformation through various creative practices. One person who has inspired me for years is Julia Cameron, the author of "The Artist's Way". Julia shares her journey of discovering a lifeline within the realm of art and self-expression during her battle with mental illness.

She embraces various creative outlets, such as writing and painting, finding solace and relief from the inner turmoil that plagued her for most of her life. The act of creation became her refuge, allowing her to confront and navigate her inner demons. With each stroke of the brush and every word she penned, she experienced a profound release, pouring out her fears, insecurities, and past traumas onto the canvas and the pages of her journals.

There is so much of Julia's journey that I can relate to, and I'm grateful for her work. She truly is guided by an Angel and has been an Angel for me.

> There is immense power in the Creative Practices. It serves as a pathway to self-discovery, healing, and unlocking a sense of purpose, joy, and connection. It has the potential to profoundly transform you, providing mental and physical relief and a deeper understanding of yourself.

What The Creative Practices Have Done For Me

- I no longer suffer for weeks or months with depression. I no longer feel completely alone in the world, disconnected and out of place. When I turn to these practices, I can transform a negative thought within 10 minutes using a creative technique that brings me joy.

- Panic attacks and overwhelming anxiety no longer consume me. I no longer define myself as a person with depression. Instead, I embrace the fact that I possess incredible skills to navigate most situations, and I want to empower you to do the same.

- I discovered many of these techniques when I was young and turned to pen and paper when I felt unable to confide in anyone. Writing became a lifeline during a time of great confusion, allowing me to truly express my emotions and leave them on the page.

- ✗ I was prescribed depression and anxiety medication around the age of 13 and used it sporadically until my late 20s when I started exploring alternative tools to manage my emotions without relying on medication.

- ♥ These tools include the practices I'm sharing with you in this book, as well as adopting a healthier food plan by eliminating refined and artificial sugars and heavily processed foods. I share all of this in my first book: "Upgradeology, Upgrade Your Food, Upgrade Your Life."

> **The Creative Practices serve as a guiding light, offering healing, self-discovery, and fulfillment. Through the power of creativity, you can transcend darkness, confront your inner demons, and find inner peace. With the support of Your Angel, you can venture into a transformative journey, unlocking your true potential and embracing a life filled with purpose and joy.**

"Art is not about thinking something up. It is the opposite - getting something down."
— Julia Cameron

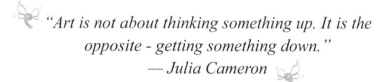

This chapter explores the power of creativity and the transformative journey it offers. Discovering unique ways to express yourself and recognize how a simple dot or a single written word can ignite your self-expression. By embracing creativity, expressing your desires, and seeking guidance from Your Angel, you can overcome self-doubt and step into your true purpose, experiencing a deep sense of fulfillment and connection. Just like a simple dot can unlock extraordinary possibilities, you are encouraged to take that courageous first step and venture into your own creative journey, knowing that you are supported by the presence and guidance of Your Angel.

What if... I embraced the creativity within myself, I wonder what would happen?

Dear Angel of Transformation, please shower me with ideas and outlets that help me heal and transform inside and out. Thank you, thank you, thank you.

Creative Practice

Dot Doodles:

- 💜 Unleash your natural creativity by drawing or painting an array of dots!

- 💜 Grab whatever art supplies you have, or just your pen or pencil. Allow yourself to have a child-like spirit and just jump in with dots of all kinds – big and small, colored in and hollow.

- 💜 Allow the dots to guide you into a place of curious creativity and self-expression. You can do it!

In the next chapter, I'll demonstrate how asking Your Angel simple questions can lead to positive changes in your life…

Whatever you're thinking about is literally like planning a future event.

— *Abraham Hicks*

Chapter 9
Squirrel-Itis

Shifting Your Focus To What You DO Want

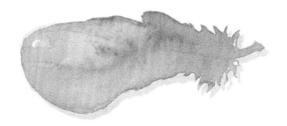

How can asking My Angel for help and guidance lead to positive changes in my life?

Purple-Quilly

In the land of fables, there was a creative soul named Purple-Quilly. She had a passion for art and a deep desire to create meaningful artwork. However, she easily got distracted by what others were doing online. She would compare herself to fellow artists, and constantly criticized her own work.

Purple-Quilly's creative journey was similar to the grasshopper in "The Ant and the Grasshopper" fable. She would jump from one artistic trend to another, never fully committing or finishing her own projects. This lack of focus left her feeling unsatisfied and stuck in a cycle of disappointment.

One day, while watching the movie "Up," Purple-Quilly noticed a scene between a dog named Dug and a mischievous little squirrel. It reminded her of her own struggle with distraction and the need to refocus on what truly mattered. Just like Dug's determination to chase the S Q U I R R E L, Purple-Quilly understood that she had to control her distractions and stay focused on enhancing her craft and creating her own artworks.

Determined to break free from this negative pattern, Purple-Quilly made a crucial decision. She disconnected from the distractions of social media, silenced the noise of outside opinions, and turned her attention inward. She chose to focus on what she did want—to create art that expressed her true self and brought her joy, instead of dwelling on what she didn't want: that constant feeling of comparison and the belief that she was falling behind.

Embracing the epiphany of Doug's struggles, Purple-Quilly would jump up and say "SQUIRREL!" every time she found herself slipping back into the old habits of scrolling and comparing. With this reminder, she committed to nurturing her own skills, mastering her techniques, and stepping into her unique style. She shifted her mindset from seeking validation to finding fulfillment in the creative practice itself.

As Purple-Quilly practiced staying focused, and letting the squirrel-itis slip away, her passion ignited like never before. She poured massive amounts of energy into her art, allowing her authentic voice to shine through. She no longer felt the need to imitate others or compare herself to their achievements. She found it easier to focus and complete the works she had started.

She found comfort and inspiration in her own artistic journey.

With each day devoted to her own body of work, Purple-Quilly experienced a deep sense of satisfaction and accomplishment. She discovered that by focusing on what she did want—finished artworks, better technical skills, and self-expression—she attracted more of it into her life.

As Purple-Quilly's artwork evolved, it touched the hearts of others. Her pieces resonated with viewers on a profound level because they were created from a place of authenticity and passion. Her art spoke volumes, telling stories of resilience, beauty, and self-discovery.

Purple-Quilly's transformation became proof of the power of focusing on one's true desires. **By shifting her attention from what she didn't want to what she did want, she unleashed a creative force within her.** Success followed in the form of stepping into personal fulfillment, growth, and a deep sense of purpose.

And so, Purple-Quilly continued to create art that spoke to her soul and began to touch the souls of others. She knew that the key to her success lay in embracing her own personal journey, practicing unwavering focus on what she wanted, and banishing the squirrel-itis of comparison, distraction, and self-doubt.

Her story became a guiding light for aspiring artists, reminding them that by directing their attention toward their true desires, they too could unlock their full potential and create a life filled with purpose, success, and joy.

And Purple-Quilly lived creatively ever after.

Focusing On What You Do Want.

These practices can help you shift your focus from what you don't want to what you do want. **This means letting go of complaining or expecting others to change.**

These practices encourage YOU to Ask Your Angel for help, but it's up to YOU to practice it daily.

You can do it, and it becomes easier and more natural the more consistent you are with it.

And… the Creative Practices help make it FUN and EASY!

You Were Born An Artist

I've heard so many people say "I'm not creative" or "I'm not an artist"…HOGWASH!

You have infinite creativity within you. It may not look like a painting or what you consider to be artistic, but it's in you. In these pages, you will discover so many creative ways to explore and express your own personal creativity. Your creativity is truly limitless!

> *"Every child is an artist. The problem is how to remain an artist once we grow up."*
> — Pablo Picasso

If you believe you're not creative or a born artist, then I'm pretty sure someone TOLD you that or made you FEEL that way when you were younger.

"If there is a voice within you that says you cannot paint, by all means paint, and that voice will be silenced." — Vincent Van Gogh

Comparison Is A Terrible Torture!

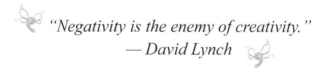

Together, let's overcome those FALSE messages and help you reclaim all of your born creativity! Being an artist isn't limited to drawing, painting, or performing. It includes cooking, gardening, creating a beautiful home, writing, doodling, crafting, and so much more. You are a one-of-a-kind work of art, and I'm here to help you embrace that truth.

"Negativity is the enemy of creativity."
— David Lynch

Here Are The Angel's Messages For You

- You are not alone! Your Angel is here for you, whether you perceive them or believe in them or not.
- You can ask for help and guidance at any time, no matter what.

- ♥ You can use any Creative Practice to help you ask and receive help, guidance, and relief.

- ♥ The more you ask, the more you receive.

- ♥ Angels love to give! They are there for you, they marvel at the growth, playfulness, learning, and sharing of their child. You are their child, and they are amazing guardians.

> **If you are someone who did not have the support of nurturing parents, take comfort in the fact that it is never too late for you to let Your Angel step into that role and offer you their unwavering love, kindness, and guidance. By fostering self-compassion and kind self-talk, you will create an environment that not only allows you to seek assistance but also opens the door for Your Angel to provide their loving support of you.**

This chapter emphasizes the power of focusing on what you DO want in order to bring it to life. Through the story of Purple-Quilly, who struggled with squirrel-itis and comparison, you learned the importance of staying focused on your own creative journey. By shifting your attention from what you don't want to what you do want, you can unleash your creative potential, find fulfillment, and create a life filled with more creativity, purpose, and joy. This chapter encourages you to practice staying focused on your desires by embracing the Creative Practices to help you on your way.

> What do you want most to do? That's what I have to keep asking myself, in the face of difficulties.
>
> — *Katherine Mansfield*

What if... I allowed myself to ask My Angel for focus and encouragement?

Dear Angel of Focus, please help me stay focused on what I truly want and shield me from distractions, especially that mischievous SQUIRREL! Let me prioritize my work and resist the urge to compare myself to others by being proud of what I've already accomplished. Thank you, thank you, thank you. Love, Purple-Quilly.

SQUIRREL-ITIS

Squirrel-itis Doodle:

- Draw what triggers your "squirrel-itis" – those distractions that pull your focus away.

- Next, write down some actionable steps to regain focus and redirect your attention to what truly matters.

This simple exercise empowers you to recognize and overcome distractions, nurturing a more concentrated and intentional mindset.

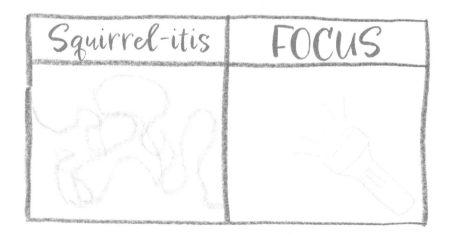

Moving on, in the next chapter, let's understand how you can feel empowered even if you've experienced abuse, neglect, or trauma…

True self-care is not bath salts and chocolate cake, it's making the choice to build a life you don't need to escape from.

— *Brianna Wiest*

Chapter 10
Breaking Free

Understanding What You Can And Can't Control

How can I feel empowered if I've been victimized?

Breaking Free

In my mid-30s, I became interested in an unconventional therapeutic practice to help with the ongoing anxiety and depression I experienced. During a session, the practitioner said something to me that had a profound impact: **"Stop being a victim."**

A weird sensation of distorted time came over me, like the long couple of seconds before an accident. It was a blunt statement, lacking further explanation, but I trusted him for his directness. Though it was like the song lyric "jagged little pill," where I found myself bewildered and deep in thought about what he said. As we went our separate ways, his words echoed relentlessly in my mind… "Stop being a Victim… Stop being a Victim… Stop being a Victim."

Until then, I had never seen myself as a victim. Past therapists would usually sympathize with my struggles, but no practitioner had ever been this straightforward with me. **I was forever changed, I questioned everything I thought and said. I began to analyze what I spoke about and thought about his words all the time… ((((((("Stop being a victim.")))))))**

It became clear that everything out of my mouth was blaming someone else for the way my life turned out or for my state of being. I realized I WAS trapped in the vicious cycle of victimhood, constantly blaming others for the current state of my life.

That moment remains etched in my memory. His words reverberated, each repetition revealing more insights. I replayed the scene, noticing the disgust and exhaustion exposed on his face as he said it. It was as if I had never truly seen myself before, unaware of a negative, destructive, and pervasive pattern that had shaped my entire existence.

After much reflection, I had to admit that it was true… I was acting like a victim. I constantly blamed others for the depression and the unfortunate events I experienced. It took time, and a lot of processing, but now I know not to go into that old story.

The moment I find myself blaming someone else for my suffering, I usually catch it and strive to do the work to understand them, understand the situation, and understand my response to the situation.

Now, I refuse to revisit that worn-out story. The more you replay a memory, the more it solidifies in your mind. It's time to create a new story.

> *"The more you think about something, the more it becomes ingrained in your brain, and the more likely it is to become your reality."*
> *— Dr. Daniel Amen*

Listen... do you hear that?

How are you speaking to yourself?

What harsh and harmful words do you constantly speak to yourself with?

Write down some of these harsh and hurtful things you say to yourself, then look at them and ask yourself, "If someone else said this to me, would they be my friend? Would they be someone I'd want to hang out with?"

If the answer is no, I wouldn't want someone to speak to me that way, **then this is your wake-up call to start shifting the way you speak to yourself.**

Your mind believes what you tell it, so if you are constantly telling yourself that you are stupid or useless, your body and mind are listening and responding to those hurtful things just as if someone else said them to you.

"Emotions are yours and you can learn to release them like freeing a bird from its cage."
— *John Assaraf*

Embracing softer self-talk and seeking assistance from Your Angel can be transformative in breaking free from negative self-talk. Here are some tools and techniques to help you.

Reframing Negative Self-Talk

Hurtful things I say to myself:

- Reframe, what kinder things can I say to myself instead?

Gosh… I'm so stupid!

- Ok, well that didn't go as planned. Let's try it again or give it a go another time. What can I do differently? Do I need to slow down, plan better, or do I need to look at this in a different light?

Just notice how you are still being honest with yourself that something didn't go well, but instead of berating yourself, you are choosing to investigate what happened which helps you make different decisions if faced with this situation again.

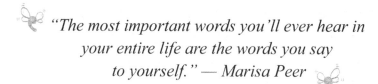

"The most important words you'll ever hear in your entire life are the words you say to yourself." — Marisa Peer

Understanding What You Can & Can't Control

When being a human in this world, it's important to understand what is in your control and what is out of your control. Here are some things to think about the next time you have an issue.

What You CAN Control

- **Your Actions:** You have control over your own behaviors, choices, and decisions. You can choose how you respond to various situations.

- **Attitude & Mindset:** Your attitude and mindset are within your control. You can choose to maintain a positive outlook, practice gratitude, and adopt an open mindset.

- **Effort & Work Ethic:** The amount of effort you put into your work, projects, or personal goals is in your control. You can choose to work diligently and with determination.

- **Time Management:** You have control over how you manage your time and prioritize tasks. Effective time management is a skill you can develop.

- **Communication:** Your words and how you communicate with others are within your control. You can choose to communicate clearly, respectfully, and empathetically.

- **Self-Care:** Taking care of your physical and mental well-being is something you can control. You can prioritize self-care activities such as movement, mindfulness, creativity, and eating nutritious foods.

What You CAN'T Control

- **Other People's Actions:** You cannot control the actions, decisions, or behaviors of other people.

- **External Circumstances:** Certain external factors, such as weather, economic conditions, or global events, are beyond your control.

- **Other People's Feelings & Reactions:** While you can influence how you interact with others, you cannot control their emotions or how they react to situations.

- **Past Events:** Events that have already occurred are in the past and cannot be changed. You can only control how you respond to the consequences of those events.

- **Natural Events:** Natural disasters, accidents, and unpredictable events are beyond your control. The only thing you can control is how you respond to them.

> **Begin to put more focus on what you CAN control. These are your own actions, thoughts, and behaviors, as well as how you respond to various situations. Understanding and accepting what you cannot control is essential for managing stress and making informed decisions. It's important to focus your energy and efforts on what is within your sphere of influence, rather than dwelling on things beyond your control.**

You can Ask Your Angel to help you focus on what you CAN control and to let go of the things you can't control.

Remember to ASK for the shift for YOU and within YOU, not others.

"Don't Take Anything Personally. Nothing others do is because of you. What others say and do is a projection of their own reality, their own dream. When you are immune to the opinions and actions of others, you won't be the victim of needless suffering." — Don Miguel Ruiz, The Four Agreements

How To Focus On The Solution?

Reframing is the process of changing or shifting your perspective on a situation or problem, allowing for a new and more positive interpretation or understanding to emerge. Reframing involves looking at something from a different angle and to find alternative meanings, possibilities, and solutions.

Sometimes just changing the way you think about the problem can help you focus and shift your way toward the solution.

- ASK yourself: What is the solution? Or… I wonder what would happen if I focused on finding the solution?
- Identify what it is you DO want and move in that direction.
- Write down the problem and then list all possible solutions without judgment. Get curious and explore with I wonder… questions.
- Focus on what you can control. Remember, you can only control yourself. Others are on their own paths, and trying to control someone else is something to look at and question what you are truly after. First, see what needs to shift in yourself.
- Shift your focus to what you can control.

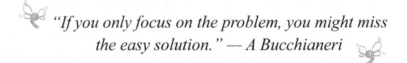

"If you only focus on the problem, you might miss the easy solution." — A Bucchianeri

If you find yourself constantly going back to the problem, start listing out all of the possible solutions you can think of. This begins to help you shift away from the problem and towards the solutions.

Once you make this list, ~~cross out~~ anything that is beyond your control and take action on something that is within your control.

Sometimes, letting go, acceptance of what is, taking a breath, journaling, or seeking guidance from someone who is solution-oriented can offer valuable insights.

> ✗ **PREVIOUS YOU:** What I don't want is - (This is Problem Focused).
>
> ♥ **CURRENT YOU:** What I do want is - (This is Solution Focused).

By focusing on the solution rather than dwelling on the problem, you can break free from the victim mindset and start moving towards empowerment and feeling like you do have control over yourself. Be sure to be aware of the language you use towards yourself. Shifting your own self-talk to kinder self-talk is a transformation you have to experience to believe.

In this chapter, I shared with you my own path of releasing the victim mentality which cracked open the door to allow in some light. It gave me the ability to respond differently, and to start using more compassionate self-talk. It's essential to reframe negative thoughts and to shift your focus toward the solution you DO want. You can always ask Your Angel for guidance to help you focus on the solution and break free from the victim mentality. Be aware of your self-talk, reframe it, and start to respond differently to situations that used to trip you up. Give it a try, you just might find it to be the most liberating practice in your life.

What if... I asked My Angel to help me focus my attention toward the solution?

Dear Angel of Solutions, let me be open to hearing from you. Let me write down my issues and then consciously focus on the solution. Let me know if I'm meant to take action, let it go, or communicate further, please let me just take the next step. Thank you, thank you, thank you!

Solution Doodling:

- Grab pen and paper, and write down the word "Solutions"

- Begin to let your pen move around the word.

- Choose doodles or symbols that represent seeking solutions for you. Consider things such as a flashlight, question marks, stars, and light bulbs. Explore your personal symbolism through this creative practice.

Solutions

In the next chapter, you will learn the secret to deepening connections with Your Angel…

Angels can turn our darkness to light, help our dreams to come true, and our worries take flight, so pass them your burdens, give them your cares, they're waiting to help you, just trust they are there.

— *Mary Jac*

Chapter 11
It's A Wonderful Life

Mastering The Art Of Asking

How can I deepen my connection with My Angel?

Angel Clarence

"It's a Wonderful Life" is a heartwarming film. The main character is George Bailey, a man who becomes deeply depressed and considers ending his life on Christmas Eve. His despair is due to financial struggles and a sense of failure. But then… an Angel named Clarence is sent to show George the profound impact he has had on the lives of those around him. Through a series of events and flashbacks, George realizes the value of his life and how his actions have touched so many people's lives in meaningful ways. This realization helps him rediscover hope, purpose, and the joy of life.

The film beautifully illustrates the transformative power of connection and community. It highlights the importance of selflessness, empathy, and the understanding that one's life is never devoid of meaning. Through George's journey, we get to witness how acts of kindness, sacrifice, and genuine human connection can pull someone out of the depths of despair. **It emphasizes the idea that even during your darkest times, there is always hope, and your life is intertwined with others in ways you may never fully comprehend.**

"It's a Wonderful Life" teaches you that your worth is not solely measured by material success or personal achievements. It reminds you that your actions, no matter how seemingly small, can have a profound ripple effect on the lives of others. By reaching out, helping those in need, and nurturing meaningful relationships, you can find purpose, fulfillment, and a renewed sense of joy. The film encourages you to cherish the present, appreciate the beauty in everyday moments, and recognize the extraordinary impact you have on the lives of those around you.

Angels possess the transformative ability to shift what you perceive as undesirable into what you truly want, but you must learn to shift your focus from complaining about what you don't want to actively asking for what you DO want, thus aligning yourself with the positive changes you seek.

Remember, you are capable of doing anything that you focus on.

 "Chop Wood, Carry Water" — Zen Proverb

IT'S A WONDERFUL LIFE

I was reminded of this fantastic quote by a lovely community member of the Art Therapeutics family. Thanks for the reminder, Kim!

Whenever a problem arises, ask Your Angel for help: HOW CAN I RESOLVE THIS?

- Ask Your Angel for the SOLUTION you seek.
- Then FOCUS on the solution, focus on what you DO want. Ask for what you DO want.
- Next, think about one simple step you can take in the direction of the solution, do it, and then let it go. Move on with your life and 'chop wood, carry water'.
- If you have no idea what the solution is, then ask for a solution to come to you.

Ask for the solution and then see if there is something you can do to work towards the solution.

"Chop wood, carry water" is a Zen proverb that emphasizes the importance of being present and focused on the tasks at hand. It originated from a famous Zen saying, "Before enlightenment, chop wood, carry water. After enlightenment, chop wood, carry water." This proverb highlights the idea that even after achieving what you want, you must still engage in everyday tasks and responsibilities.

If the solution is out of your control, then ask to let go of the problem and the burden of thinking about it.

Then you can ask Your Angel to help you let go and move on.

Try this exercise for one month, and you will see significant changes. Remember, if you focus on the problem, the problem will be what you are experiencing; the problem will occupy your mind.

If you SHIFT your focus to ASKING for a SOLUTION, you will begin to see more possible solutions and fewer problems."

What if asking Your Angel for what you want will bring in positive changes into your life?

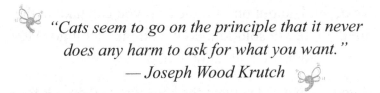

"Cats seem to go on the principle that it never does any harm to ask for what you want."
— Joseph Wood Krutch

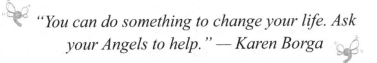

"You can do something to change your life. Ask your Angels to help." — Karen Borga

Mastering The Art Of Asking

In 2020, I discovered again that I needed help, but not from a doctor or even a therapist, as I had tried those many times in the past. The help I needed could only be found by going within and asking My Angel for help.

And when this realization truly sank in, everything changed!

I finally figured out that I didn't need junk food, drugs, alcohol, movie binging, countless hours of scrolling, shopping, or even someone to confide in about my problems. What I needed was an inside fix—the ones I found that only My Angel could help me with.

> **Some may refer to this force as God, Spirit, Light, The Universe, etc… I call it An Angel. You can call it whatever resonates with you.**

Ask Your Angel (i.e. God, Spirit, Light, Universe, etc…) for what you want!

Asking for what you want is similar to putting an address into your GPS because both require you to have a clear goal or destination in mind. Just as a GPS needs to know the exact location so that it can give you the best route, asking Your Angel for what you want requires you to clarify your desired outcome and then ask for it.

Once you have a clear goal in mind, ask Your Angel to help you. Trust that Your Angel is there for you and that Your Angel wants to help you. **Angels are always listening and waiting for you to ask**. Remember, they are messengers and when you begin to do this practice frequently, you will hear their messages more and more clearly.

Asking for help can sometimes feel difficult or uncomfortable, but it's important to remember that you don't have to do everything on your own. You have Your Angel ready to support you and guide you on your journey.

It's also important to be open to receiving the help that Your Angel provides. Sometimes the help you receive may not be exactly what you expected, but it's important to trust that it just might be exactly what you need in that moment.

As with anything in this book, it's just a suggestion. Try it on like you would a new shirt and see if it fits. If so, take it as your own, if not, leave it for someone else.

> **The Ask & Action Method**
> → Ask for what you want.
> → Ask for what you need to do to get there.
> → Ask for the willingness to do it.
> → Take action, no matter how small!

Any action, some small action that lets Your Angel know that you are serious about this ask. The action is usually found in what you are willing to do for whatever it is you want.

 "The journey of a thousand miles begins with one step." — Lao Tzu

IT'S A WONDERFUL LIFE

EXAMPLE OF THE ASK AND ACTION METHOD:

- **Ask For What You Want:** Angel, I want to stop eating so late at night.

- **Ask For What You Need To Do To Get There:** Angel, I need to eat a solid breakfast, lunch, and dinner so that I'm not wanting to eat all evening because I haven't eaten enough during the day.

- **Ask For The Willingness To Do What Needs To Be Done:** Angel, please give me the willingness to prepare healthy meals throughout the day so that I feel satisfied by the time evening comes.

- **Take Action:** I will write out my food plan for tomorrow so that I have breakfast, lunch, and dinner planned out.

Remember, you have the power to transform your life, and seeking assistance from Your Angel is a significant step in that direction. Trust your intuition, trust their guidance, and believe in yourself. You can do this!

> *"If you can't fly, then run, if you can't run, then walk, if you can't walk, then crawl, but whatever you do, you have to keep moving forward."*
> — *Martin Luther King, Jr.*

In this chapter, we focus the flashlight on the power of asking for help from Your Angel. You are encouraged to be clear about your goals, ask Your Angel for assistance, trust in their guidance, and take any action, no matter how small toward your desires.

What if... I possess all the tools within me to transform my life and what if I asked My Angel for solutions?

Dear Angel of Solutions, please let me ask for your help in times of need, not because I am feeling weak or powerless, but because there is strength and power in the asking as I know you will provide a solution for me, now or in the future. Thank you, thank you, thank you.

IT'S A WONDERFUL LIFE

Reflection Doodle:

- Ask Your Angel for something you want by writing it down.

- Begin to write or doodle around what you are Asking for, just see where it takes you.

- Ask yourself, what chopping of wood and carrying of water do I think would benefit this ask?

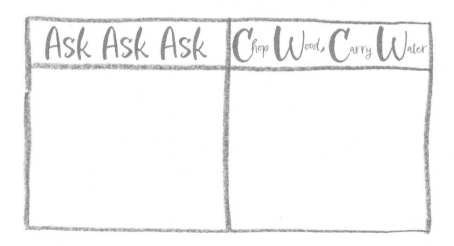

In the next chapter, you'll learn about mindfulness in some different and not-so-obvious places…

Wherever you are, be there totally. If you find your here and now intolerable and it makes you unhappy, you have three options: remove yourself from the situation, change it, or accept it totally.

— *Eckhart Tolle*

Chapter 12

Meditation In A Strange Place

Mindfulness And Shaking It Off

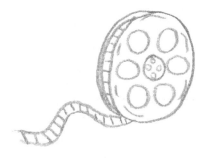

How can I be more mindful about what I do, say, and think?

Meditation In A Strange Place

One damp and rainy day in Portland, Oregon, around 2008, I found myself browsing through the meditation section of a bookstore. Surprisingly, I stumbled upon a book authored by David Lynch. I thought this must be a different David Lynch than the Eraserhead, Blue Velvet, and Twin Peaks David Lynch that I was familiar with. The title was "Catching the Big Fish"… when I opened the book, oh my gosh—it WAS Him!

In a world where mindfulness and meditation are often associated with that certain look of yogis and spiritual teachers, the idea of a cigarette-smoking, surrealist movie maker embracing meditation dropped my jaw! David Lynch shattered the stereotype and showcased that mindfulness can benefit anyone, regardless of their background or artistic inclinations.

As I devoured the pages of David's book, I was captivated by his unique perspective on using meditation to enhance creativity. He embraced his own dance with darkness, fully stepping into his mind-bending nature, instead of conforming to the image of a spiritual guru. **Through the gifts of mindfulness and meditation, David Lynch found a pathway to creative fulfillment, releasing his anger, and as a result, had better film crews because he treated them with respect instead of yelling at them, further enhancing his artistic excellence.**

What impressed me most was the simplicity of his practice. Despite his busy schedule and movie-making lifestyle, he dedicated just 20 minutes a day, a few times a day to meditation. In those moments of stillness, he tapped into a wellspring of creativity and clarity, allowing his imagination to flow freely and release the anger that used to take over him.

As I closed his book, I felt a profound sense of inspiration from David Lynch's journey. **His willingness to embrace meditation as a tool for self-exploration and creative expression reminded me of the boundless potential within each of us.** It motivated me to incorporate mindfulness even more into my own life, not only for inner peace but also as a means to unlock and embrace my own dark art and creative potential.

Mr. Mulholland Drive's (David Lynch) story serves as a powerful reminder that mindfulness knows no boundaries. **Practicing mindfulness** can be a catalyst for personal transformation and artistic growth. David Lynch's journey is proof of the vast possibilities that arise when you embrace your unique paths and harness the gifts of meditation and mindfulness to enhance your life and your creative endeavors.

> Ideas are like fish. If you want to catch little fish, you can stay in the shallow water. But if you want to catch the big fish, you've got to go deeper.
>
> *— David Lynch*

Writing out a meditation would defeat the purpose since it's best to have your eyes closed for the true sense of this particular definition of meditation, so I've provided a supplemental and simple meditation focused on relaxation and releasing anxiety. It's easy. Guided meditations are the best way to start out if you have never meditated before or if you find meditating on your own difficult. **To download your Meditation, go to:** www.NicoleWhiteWellness.com

Take A Deep Breath

I know, I know, talking about the breath and mindfulness may seem cliché by now, but it truly works!

As a non-smoker for over 23 years, I've come to realize what I was truly seeking during those cigarette breaks—it was a moment to take a deep breath and to tell my nervous system that everything will be okay.

Taking a deep breath is a remarkable practice that holds countless benefits for your overall well-being. Within the rhythm of your breath is a powerful tool, always present and readily available, offering you the gift of calm-strength. In the moments when life just feels too overwhelming or chaotic, you possess the ability to regain control simply by taking a few deep breaths.

This action, so simple and yet so profound, allows you to find your center, anchoring yourself in the present moment. It can truly be a sanctuary of tranquility that you can embrace discreetly without anyone else even noticing.

> - **Inhaling deeply**, you draw in revitalizing energy, filling your lungs with life's vital essence.
> - As you **Exhale**, ask yourself to release any tension, stress, or anything that doesn't serve you well.
> - As you **Inhale**, breathe in and ask for what you need.
> - With the **Exhale**... letting go.

Each breath carries with it a quiet reminder that you are capable of finding peace amidst the turbulence of life.

Embrace the gift of your breath, for it is a nurturing companion, ever faithful and supportive.

Let its gentle rhythm guide you toward a calm and grounded state, enabling you to move through challenges with clarity and more ease.

> **Breathe deeply, Your Angel says, and discover the transformative power that lies within this simple act of being present.**

Simple Breathing Techniques

→ Stop and notice your body and the racing of your mind.

→ Take a deep breath in. Imagine Your Angel breathing deeply with you.

← Exhale fully.

→ Breathe in deeply once again.

← Allow the exhale to happen naturally.

→ Take another deep breath in.

← As you exhale, let go in your shoulders, face, or anywhere you feel tension. And consciously notice the difference.

→ Rinse and Repeat. Do this multiple times until you truly feel calm and grounded… it truly won't take long.

Or Simply:

→ **INHALE:** What it is you DO want

← **EXHALE:** Whatever doesn't serve you well

The Shake It Off Method

If you've ever spent time with a dog, what is something they do all the time?

They SHAKE!!!

- Dogs wake up, stretch, and shake.
- After a walk, they shake.
- When they sense sudden danger, they freeze and then shake when they feel safe again.
- Animals intuitively know how to release stress and trauma through shaking!

Shaking isn't just for animals; it's good for you too! When you shake your body, it can help you feel better in so many ways.

Let's take a cue from Taylor Swift and her song "Shake It Off" because she's onto something important!

"Cause the players gonna
play, play, play, play, play
And the haters gonna
hate, hate, hate, hate, hate
Baby, I'm just gonna
shake, shake, shake, shake, shake
I shake it off, I shake it off"

- Shaking helps you relax and reduce stress. This happens because shaking activates a part of your nervous system that calms you down. It's like telling your body it's okay to take a break.

- Shaking gets your blood moving better, which means your muscles and organs get more oxygen and nutrients. This can make you feel more energetic.

- Shaking can make your immune system stronger by improving the flow of a special fluid called lymph. It's like giving your body's defense system a little boost. Also, when you shake, you can let out built-up feelings and tension, like letting the air out of a balloon. It helps you feel more connected to your body and emotions.

- Shaking can be like a safety valve for your emotions, helping you release them before they turn into physical pain or stress. Think about the release valve on a pressure cooker. So, don't be surprised if you find yourself feeling much better after a really good shake!

Let me tell you about a client of mine who reached out because she was dealing with a highly stressful situation, and I introduced her to the 'Shake It Off Method.' When we followed up later that day, she informed me that it had significantly helped her alleviate stress. She was pleasantly surprised by how effectively and rapidly it worked for her.

Over the years, I've adopted this practice of shaking. If any kind of stressful or shocking event happens, I will go where I feel safe and/or alone and begin to shake with my entire body. I'll let sounds come out and do anything from tremble to full-out shaking. Sometimes that's not enough and so then I'll start to make deep "huh" sounds while exhaling and if that's not enough, I'll let myself scream!

All of this starts to move the emotion or event out of your body, releasing it before it becomes trapped emotions that all too often end up as tension or pain somewhere in the body – tight shoulders or neck, stiff or painful back… or the all notorious headache or migraine! If this starts to happen to you, adopt the "Shaking It Off Method" and feel how instantly the relief can be.

Gratitude

Gratitude is a simple way to genuinely enrich and improve your life! Numerous studies and books have shown that merely listing three things you're grateful for in the morning and before bed can reduce feelings of sadness, depression, stress, and anxiety. Gratitude can also improve your sleep and enhance your self-confidence by helping you feel more connected to your life and aware that there are still so many things in the world to be thankful and grateful for.

The best part is that it's REALLY EASY! Just write down or say out loud three things that you're thankful or grateful for in the morning and in the evening.

Your GRATITUDES Can Be Simple, Such As:

I'm grateful for my family, my dog, and my friends.

OR, They Can Be As Detailed As You Like:

I appreciate the beautiful sunset I witnessed this evening with all of its glorious colors and light.

I'm thankful for the ability to concentrate on my project today. I'm grateful for the vacation to the beach that I'm planning for next year.

Go ahead, try it out now…

I'm Grateful for:

1. …

2. …

3. …

Saying Thank You!

Saying "Thank You" is a powerful lesson I stumbled upon in my early thirties, by accident. This little tool has the potential to significantly boost your self-esteem and create stronger connections with those around you.

Struggling to receive compliments??? You might relate to scenarios like these:

Compliment Giver: "I really love that shirt, it looks great on you!"
Me: "Oh, this old thing, it's just what I picked out this morning. I think it just covers up the fat."

Compliment Giver: "You're really nice for helping me today, thank you so much!"
Me: "It's the least I could do; I'm pretty lazy, so it's good to get something done today."

When you can't accept a compliment, you're essentially turning it away, as if someone had crafted a homemade gift for you and you tossed it in the trash right in front of them. Rejecting a compliment, especially from someone you care about, is actually quite rude! Accepting the compliment, however, is a gift in return.

I used to be that person who would always try to deflect a compliment. But in my early thirties, a pair of glasses my mom gifted me changed my perspective for the better. While those glasses have long since broken, the lesson they taught me was invaluable and lives on…

The Magic Of Saying "Thank You."

As I wore my new, incredibly cool glasses, people noticed them and began complimenting them. At first, I was unsure how to respond. I was usually reserved and not used to such attention. Then, I had a little conversation with myself, a 'Come

To Angel' moment, if you will. It went something like this: "These glasses are really awesome, and I picked them because I absolutely love them. When someone compliments them, they're not really complimenting me, but the glasses. So, why not just say thank you?"

As I started saying "Thank you" in response to the compliments they (the glasses) received, something remarkable happened within me. I realized how much better it felt to simply accept the compliment rather than trying to reject it with an excuse. I remember leaving the grocery store after someone complimented the glasses when it clicked, it instilled in me the habit of acknowledging compliments with gratitude.

This is about what it looks like when someone compliments me now…

Compliment Giver: "This chocolate you made is delicious, thank you."

Me inside my compliment-rejecting mind: "Ohhhh… this batch isn't as good as what I've made before; I should make some improvements, I know I can do better. They really didn't get the best chocolate I know I can make, ugh."

Me Out Loud: "Thank you so much; I really appreciate you saying that."

Try it for yourself.

Pay attention to how you feel when someone compliments you. Go through the inner compliment-rejecting dialogue, and then make an effort to **squeeeeeeeeeeeeeze** out a "Thank you."

Another little 'Angel Trick' is to reciprocate with a compliment. In the previous example, I not only said "Thank you" but also added, "I appreciate you saying that." This helps bridge the gap when you're uncomfortable with compliments, reminding you to express more gratitude and share appreciation in return.

This approach helps you when you are hesitant to accept positive attention and it also encourages others to give you more compliments. I noticed that by frequently rejecting compliments, people would eventually stop giving them. **You actually train people how to treat you through your responses.**

Give it some thought, see what resonates with you, and consider adopting this simple practice of accepting compliments and saying "Thank You" when someone does. You'll find yourself naturally giving more compliments as well. Also, after accepting a compliment, you can always say something like "I appreciate you saying that" or "I appreciate you noticing that." This can help neutralize your internal state as it gets used to receiving compliments and is also a way to appreciate the person appreciating you.

You are accepting the gift of the compliment they gave you, and in return, you express how much you appreciate their appreciation… and then it becomes a beautiful appreciation of appreciation moment… how beautiful is that!!!

Moving Meditations

Meditation doesn't always have to be about sitting still. Meditation can also be a moving meditation, such as walking, yoga, qigong, being in nature, star gazing, nature gazing, a bath, focusing on your breath, and other slow mindful practices.

Moving Meditations can also be quick like listening to music you love and dancing. Cleaning can also be a Moving Meditation.

While traditional meditation is incredible and offers numerous benefits, there are other forms of meditation worth exploring:

Art can be a form of meditation, Writing can be a form of meditation.

Sometimes, even driving on the open road can become a meditative experience.

When you feel overwhelmed, remember to Take a Deep Breath, Shake it Off, and create distance from the stressful environment whenever possible. Additionally, you can always turn to Your Angel for assistance in navigating these practices.

Adopt the mindfulness practices that resonate with you. You'll be amazed at the positive shifts that happen for you.

Finally, don't hesitate to ask Your Angel for help in cultivating mindfulness. They are there to support you on this journey of self-discovery and awareness.

"Intuition is the key to everything, in painting, filmmaking, business - everything. I think you could have an intellectual ability, but if you can sharpen your intuition, which they say is emotion and intellect joining together, then a knowingness occurs." — David Lynch

This chapter shares something so very wonderful in that **you don't have to look the part to play the part you want.** You can create your own ways of releasing stress through breathing, shaking, and meditative practices.

Embracing your personal preference, and asking for the help that works for you and your lifestyle.

The meditative state doesn't have to resemble a bearded guy in a white robe sitting cross-legged and still. There are numerous ways you can embrace mindfulness practices to help you tune in and transform your life for the better.

You always get to ask Your Angel to help you find your own way. You can truly turn your darkness into light and manifest your dreams when you trust and seek the guidance of Your Angel and open yourself up to their messages and guidance.

Remember your meditation download at www.NicoleWhiteWellness.com

www.NicoleWhiteWellness.com

What if... I hold the power within me to be more present and fulfilled, and all I have to do is focus mindfully on what I want to do?

Dear Angel of Mindfulness, please help me stay mindful and aware when the world and its shenanigans do what they always seem to do. Please remind me to Shake It Off and take deep breaths throughout the day. Assist me in keeping a positive and mindful attitude while navigating my thoughts, actions, and journey in this world. Angel, please help me create time for my meditative art practices, allowing me to be fully present and at peace in this moment and throughout the day. Let me tap into that deep well of intuition when I need it. I am deeply grateful for your guidance. Thank you, thank you, thank you.

MEDITATION IN A STRANGE PLACE

Mindfulness Doodle:

- Think about a mindfulness practice that you either engage in now or would like to begin practicing. What benefits do you anticipate they will bring to you?

- Doodle, cut out pictures, and/or write about what benefits you anticipate they will bring to you.

In the upcoming chapter, you'll learn why it is you unintentionally hurt yourself and how to stop it…

Don't speak negatively about yourself, not even as a joke. Your body doesn't know the difference.

Words are energy and they cast spells, that's why it's called spelling. Change the way you speak about yourself, and you can change your life.

— *Bruce Lee*

Chapter 13
The Secret Sauce

Creating Compassionate Self-Talk

How can I change when I don't even know that I'm hurting myself?

→ **Hurt people hurt people.** ←
Sometimes hurt people hurt other people.
Sometimes hurt people hurt themselves.

Read that again.

Alone

One day, I woke up and realized that I was friendless in terms of tight-knit friendships and was estranged from my family. I had pushed so many people out of my life, never giving them a chance to get close to me. I always found excuses for why they wouldn't like me or why I wouldn't like them, convincing myself not to even try. My days were spent alone, engrossed in mind-spinning self-criticism, writing about all of my "problems," drawing and painting the aloneness I felt. The artwork grew darker, reflecting my inner thoughts and the bleak world I had created for myself. My nickname was Raven because I always wore black, a habit I had adopted since my teenage years.

Initially, I wore black to protect myself from bullies. But over time, it became a part of my identity. As a child, I was said to be playful and silly, often wearing mismatched socks and clothes that clashed just for fun. However, the bullying at school changed me. I gradually withdrew, wearing all black and falling silent. Yet, the negative self-talk within me never ceased. In fact, it only intensified.

Strangely, wearing black and isolating myself seemed to deter the bullies, but it also made good people wary of me. I was someone who had gone from being outwardly silly to deeply quiet and disturbed. I remember a cousin of mine said that I was "unapproachable." The harsh words I spoke to myself perpetuated my isolation and took a toll on my well-being.

This pattern persisted until my thirties. Then, one day, I had a wake-up call. I was at home, sitting in meditation, and heard a voice—I now believe it was My Angel—that said, "Enough… Stop wearing black!!!"

This moment shook me, but it also prompted me to reflect on my actions and the darkness that had consumed me. Removing the physical darkness from my appearance was just the beginning; I also had to confront the darkness within.

Gradually, I realized how I was harming myself, perpetuating the loneliness and isolation. It was time for a change. I was determined to connect with the world, to find friends, love, and a sense of community and belonging. It wasn't an easy journey, but what helped me the most was changing the way I spoke to myself.

By softening my self-talk, by speaking to myself in the way I wanted to be spoken to as a child, I gradually released a ton of negativity. The transformation brought more lightness and ease into my life. It no longer felt like the world was against me, and I no longer felt completely alone. Opening myself up to kinder and truer words paved the way for deep relationships, new friendships, and a sense of adventure. It took time and effort, but the power of shifting how I spoke to myself was truly transformative for me.

> *"Pay close attention to the particular thoughts you use to deprive yourself of happiness."*
> — *Byron Katie*

The way you speak to yourself has a profound impact on your health and well-being! Pay close attention to the harsh and hurtful words you repeatedly tell yourself and begin to soften them, to change them, to reframe them into encouraging words. **This is the most profound act you can embody to transform your life, and Your Angel is here to help you.**

"The most important words you'll ever hear in your entire life are the words you say to yourself." — Marisa Peer

Treasures and seemingly miracles will appear when you begin to use gentle and loving words towards yourself. You have the power to nurture your spirit and shape your world with your words!

"You must say I AM ENOUGH constantly, say it out loud, say it with feeling, say it like you mean it, and say it over and over again and do so for weeks until it sinks in and replaces the feeling that you are not enough which may be holding you back." — Marisa Peer

Self-criticism is downright hazardous to your health!

Did you know that self-criticism leads to a lower self-image and a constant feeling of inadequacy? It tears apart your self-esteem and prevents you from believing in yourself. **Self-criticism is one of the biggest forms of stress, anxiety, and depression.** It creates a perpetual cycle of negative thoughts and emotions that can be paralyzing and hinder your ability to truly care for yourself. So the secret sauce is… Speaking Kindly To Yourself.

 "R.E.S.P.E.C.T" — Aretha Franklin

Respect Yourself By Speaking Compassionately To Yourself

You deserve to treat yourself with kindness and respect. Your self-esteem is often shaped by your experiences and how others have treated you. However, it's important to remember that **hurt people tend to hurt people.. and in my case, and perhaps yours, it's you who continues to hurt yourself.**

Your negative self-perception is often a learned pattern that can be transformed for the better. Let's explore several ways to begin nurturing your self-talk in compassionate ways that will empower you to embrace your true worth and break free from the cycle of self-criticism and self-harm.

"Your brain is like a supercomputer, and your self-talk is the program it will run." — Jim Kwik

Self-forgiveness is something you've probably heard about, and often it seems like the most difficult thing to do. There you are in your mind, replaying and replaying something you feel you did wrong, should have done differently, or didn't address at all. You feel the weight of the world, imprisoning yourself more than someone who has spent 30 years in prison. This is a habit, but breaking free from this self-harming pattern will bring you a remarkable transformation in your life. No matter what you've done, as long as you are willing to turn it around, learn from your mistakes, and make amends if necessary, you deserve inner peace just like anyone else.

Sometimes, those who are hardest on themselves are good people who struggle to forgive themselves for making a mistake. That's why it's called a mistake—what if it's truly just a lesson in what to do and what not to do in the future? **Consider genius inventors like Tesla and countless others; they had to make so many mistakes to learn what works and what doesn't.**

If you refrain from doing anything in this world because you're afraid of making more mistakes, you won't experience the true wonder of living and exploration this world has to offer.

> **We are all here fumbling around and figuring things out as we go... I believe that's called being human!**

 "Each of us has a three-year-old child within us, and we often spend most of our time yelling at that kid in ourselves. Then we wonder why our lives don't work." — Louise Hay

> **Here are several ways to think about the harsh and hurtful things you say to yourself and to begin reframing them, softening them, and using kinder self-talk to build yourself up!**

Reflecting and Curiosity

Take a moment to notice when you're being hard on yourself or negatively judging yourself. Pause and reflect on these thoughts and emotions. Ask yourself, "Does this way of thinking truly benefit me?" By bringing curiosity and awareness to your self-critical habits, you open the door to understanding and then changing them.

Negative self-talk: "Geeeeeze (keeping it clean here), I'm such a failure. I always mess things up. I can't seem to do anything right., I'm just a big nincompoop!"

- **Reframed positive thoughts:** "Hey, you know what? We all make mistakes, every single one of us! It's just a part of being human. Inventors have to make mistakes because then they are one step closer to figuring things out. What can I learn from having a curious mind like an inventor and then figure out how to do this, or handle this better or differently next time?"

  - **EXAMPLE: Instead of beating yourself up for a mistake, you can reflect on what went wrong, learn from it, and write down how you would do it differently next time.. just like an inventor!**

Bring in Your Angel, and ask her to help you!

Dear Angel, I feel like I really messed things up again and my thoughts make me think that I can't do anything right. Please take these negative thoughts from me and instead

help me learn from my actions so that I can do things differently next time. Help me know that I'm capable of learning and growing and that I won't always feel this way. Please help me be open and curious so that I can be kinder to myself. Please let me think like an inventor would, knowing that mistakes are just stepping stones to figuring it out! Thank you, thank you, thank you.

How to do this…

- → Write down how you feel.
- → Explain to Your Angel why you feel this way.
- → Consider how an inventor would view this issue.
- → Reframe your negative thoughts to softer, kinder, and encouraging words to and about yourself.
- → If this is something that happens often, write down ways you can respond differently next time.
- → Practice, and speak out loud, how you would act or respond differently. This way, you will be prepared if there is a next time.

"Whatever you believe about yourself on the inside, is what will manifest on the outside."
— *John Assaraf*

Treating Yourself With Kindness And Understanding
Just as you would extend kindness and understanding to your younger self or someone you deeply care about, it's important to do the same for yourself.

Begin speaking to yourself in the way you wished someone would have spoken to you when you were a child.

Begin using nurturing and supportive language towards yourself.

Old negative self-talk: "I'm so (bleeeeepin) stupid. I can't believe I made that mistake… Again!"

- **Reframed positive thoughts:** "Hey, don't be too hard on yourself. We all have moments where things don't go as planned. It's okay. We'll figure it out and move forward."

    - **EXAMPLE: Instead of berating yourself for something that didn't go your way, dissect it, ask yourself what the pattern is, write it down, and ask yourself what you could do differently next time. Remind yourself that it's a learning opportunity and treat yourself with kindness and encouragement, just as you would a young person or a close friend.**

Dear Angel, I'm being really hard on myself and calling myself stupid for making a mistake. Please help me replace these negative thoughts with wonder, curiosity, and self-understanding. Please guide me to speak to myself with the same compassion I would offer to a dear friend or my younger self. Help me embrace and practice the nurturing and supportive voice within me. Thank you, thank you, thank you.

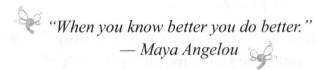

"When you know better you do better."
— *Maya Angelou*

How to do this…

→ Analyze what happened and write it down.

→ Write about the feelings you have about what happened and the outcome.

→ **Write down how you would speak to someone you love and adore if this happened to them.**

→ If applicable, **write down how you could handle this differently in the future.** Or what it would feel like to truly forgive yourself or others for what happened.

→ **THEN, take those softer and more compassionate words (you would say to a loved one) write them down, and say those kinder words to yourself.**

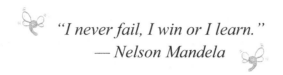

"I never fail, I win or I learn."
— *Nelson Mandela*

Focusing On Your Strengths

Everyone has strengths, and when you focus on your strengths, you cultivate a more curious and positive mindset which creates a stronger foundation for self-compassion.

Focus on your strengths, and you will notice that you begin to feel more empowered with a can-do attitude! When you feel better about yourself, you can bring in more curiosity and wonder about problem areas and how to resolve them.

Everyone has problems, and everyone has weaknesses. This includes you, me, and Everyone!

Take time to acknowledge your situation, recognize your strengths, and celebrate your past accomplishments.

Negative self-talk: "I'm not good at anything. I have no talent, I'll never be good enough, I'm such a disappointment."

- **Reframed positive thoughts:** "Listen, my friend, you are more than enough, everyone makes mistakes. Don't compare yourself to others. You have unique strengths and qualities that make you, you!"

  - **EXAMPLE: Instead of focusing on what you feel you lack, you can acknowledge your strengths, and write down how you can use them to help you focus on finding the solution.**

Dear Angel, I often feel like I'm not good at anything. Please help me open my mind and recognize my unique strengths and abilities. Guide me to acknowledge my strengths, celebrate my past accomplishments, and cultivate a more curious and positive mindset. Help me appreciate the strengths I have and use them to build a foundation for self-compassion and therefore greater self-esteem and feeling more joy and happiness in my life. Thank you, thank you, thank you.

How to do this…

- What activities make you feel energized and satisfied?

- What do others say about you? Think about the positive feedback and compliments you've received from others.

- Go into **detail** about the things you've accomplished: (Passion projects, school, work, relationships, community, creativity, your home, etc…).

- **Write out the things you know you are good at, your accomplishments, and positive feedback you've received from others on a piece of paper.**

- **Keep this list handy and read it daily.** You will find it easier to begin focusing more on your strengths.

"Some days your harshest critic will visit you in the mirror. Wave, smile, and send it love, then go kick some ass." — Sean Stephenson

These examples are meant to illustrate how negative self-talk can be reframed into more positive, truthful, and

empowering thoughts. It's important to personalize these reframed thoughts to align with your own experiences and desires. Ask Your Angel to help, she is always there for you!

Go ahead, give it a try... start with just one kind thing that you can say to yourself.

This is a **practice**, something new perhaps. **The more you practice speaking kinder to yourself, the quicker it will become familiar, so much easier to do consistently.**

Let it be awkward and weird at first... just like anything you do often, it will soon become comfortable and familiar!

Write these things down and engage with them often. Here is some space for that:

Kind Things You can begin to say to yourself:

    I am ...

"The most powerful relationship you will ever have is the relationship with yourself."
— *Diane von Furstenberg*

Begin to practice speaking to yourself more compassionately. Don't be shy, you can Ask Your Angel to help you do this. This alone will be the most transformative journey you can take. You will feel better in all areas of your life and be able to cultivate so much more creativity and joy in all you do.

The Importance Of "Yet"

Let's explore the importance of the word "Yet." This simple and transformative mindset shift involves approaching what you feel you can't currently do with the understanding that you may not have achieved something **YET!** However, with practice and determination, you DO have the potential to do it in the future!

The word "yet" can be an incredibly powerful tool in reframing negative self-talk into more positive self-talk. By adding in the word "yet" at the end of a negative statement, you begin to leave room for self-discovery, reflection, and improvement.

Example:

- ✗ **PREVIOUS YOU:** "I can't do this."
- ♥ **CURRENT YOU:** "I can't do this… YET."

By making it familiar to add in the word "yet" to the end of a negative statement, you are using an empowering tool to reframe your mindset from something closed and fixed into an open and expansive mindset.

THE SECRET SAUCE

Remember Beginner's Mind and Curiosity. It can help you build resilience, motivation, and a positive attitude toward challenges and the way you speak and feel towards yourself.

So give it a try...

> **List a few things here you want to accomplish, things you find yourself saying you are not good at, and then put "YET" at the end of that statement.**
>
> ❤ I'm not good at _____ YET.
>
> ❤ I'm not good at _____ YET.
>
> ❤ I'm not good at _____ YET.

This quote is worth repeating over and over again!

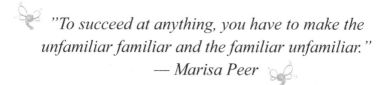

> *"To succeed at anything, you have to make the unfamiliar familiar and the familiar unfamiliar."*
> — *Marisa Peer*

If someone said they didn't have time to read this book, but truly wants the benefits from it and I could only offer up one chapter... this would be that chapter.

Let these words permeate your soul like rainwater sinking into dry earth, nurturing your roots and fostering an open mind and curiosity. Learn to reparent yourself with compassionate self-talk. Speaking to yourself as you wished to be spoken to as that child. Revisit this chapter, dog-ear the page, and let it become an unwavering guiding light.

> *"Remember, you have been criticizing yourself for years and it hasn't worked. Try approving of yourself and see what happens."* — Louise Hay

In this chapter, I'm asking you to embrace the transformative power of self-compassion, for it holds the key to a happier and more fulfilled life. Remember that hurt people hurt people, and in my case, my feeling hurt caused me to hurt myself more.

Challenge and reframe your self-talk, and you'll discover a profound shift in your overall well-being. Seek guidance from Your Angel, ask her to speak kindly to you, and teach you how to do the same for yourself.

Let this lesson sink in deeply, put it into practice immediately, stumble through it awkwardly, and allow yourself to be a beginner at it. Become open and curious about your self-talk, and notice that as you speak kinder to yourself, your life begins to transform in the most amazing ways you probably never even thought possible. **I'd recommend revisiting this chapter often… as it is the secret sauce to enriching your life and personal transformation.**

Remember, you have been criticizing yourself for years and it hasn't worked. Try approving of yourself and see what happens.

— *Louise Hay*

What if... I asked My Angel to help me focus on what I'm good at and to speak with encouragement and kindness to myself?

Dear Angel of Self-Compassion, please help me take this chapter to heart and deepen my commitment to compassionate self-talk, even in the most challenging of times. Allow me to know that anything I want to do is available to me if I include positive self-talk, a curious mind, and "YET" to the things I am not YET good at. Please also make this fun and easy. Thank you, thank you, thank you.

THE SECRET SAUCE

Selfie Doodle:

- Begin by writing, drawing, or doodling your name on paper.

- Surround your name with hearts and symbols of love, care, and positivity.

- Next, write down three kind and compassionate things you can incorporate into your daily self-talk. Embracing kind and compassionate self-talk creates a much more positive and loving inner dialogue.

1.

2.

3.

And traveling into the next chapter, I think this just might hit a funny bone for you…

Humor is the great thing, the saving thing after all. The minute it crops up, all our hardnesses yield, all our irritations and resentments flit away, and a sunny spirit takes their place.

— *Mark Twain*

Chapter 14
Finding Funny

The Benefits Of Humor

Ha ha
HA ha
HA ha Ha
ha HA
ha

What if some of the things I take so seriously are really quite funny and not worth stressing about?

Humor

I did a silly thing many years back. I took a Laughter Yoga Training. Yup, that's a thing and I'm always interested in more ways to bring in nurturing and healthy habits! I know the power of laughter, so even though it looked and sounded goofy, I was game!

Laughter yoga is where people intentionally laugh together, even if there's nothing funny happening. It combines laughter with deep breathing and movement. As you practice Laughter Yoga, you start feeling happier and the stress seems to just fall away. The benefits include feeling happier, less stressed, and a better sense of well-being. It creates a stronger immune system by getting more oxygen into your body, and you get to make new friends because you're laughing together. It's a fun and easy way to improve your health and happiness through laughter and community.

What do you call someone who doesn't have a body and doesn't have a nose? Nobody knows.

WHO KNEW that in 2020, the world would mostly shut down and that many of us would find ourselves grappling with whether or not to continue on.

Enter… my laughter yoga buddies! We would have a 15-minute Laughter video session every Monday to Friday. It was truly a lifeline. The power and community we created was immense. Those 15 minutes early in the morning completely shifted everything. I'm not sure how most of us would have survived without it. I am grateful for laughter and especially grateful for laughter yoga!

> *"Laughter is one of the best medicines around for relieving stress and for creating a more healthy spirit. And, one of the greatest aspects is that it is totally free and can be done by anyone."*
> — *Byron Pulsifer*

Another little story to the power of laughter, I remember when I hurt my back pretty badly and decided to watch a funny movie. In one part, I laughed so hard that I just forgot all about my back for a while. When I got up after the movie, something had shifted, and I swear the pain had lessened. So I gave a big thank you to Jim Carrey for helping me out that night. I said it out loud like I would to My Angel… he's Angel Jim to me. Thank You Angel Jim!

Laugh when you can. Instead of watching horror movies, the news (which is like a horror movie), dramas, or harsh action films, begin to watch comedians, funny movies, feel-good movies, nature shows, or inspirational movies. Surround yourself with humor, and let Your Angel help infuse your atmosphere with lightheartedness and joy.

"We don't laugh because we feel good, we feel good because we laugh." — Bob Ross

You Are What You Put In Or Allow In Your Atmosphere

If you put fear and drama in your atmosphere, that is how your brain will think. If you put light-hearted humor in, that is how your brain will be wired. Call upon Your Angel to guide you in filling your surroundings with positivity and humor.

Humor reduces stress and tension by releasing the relaxation response in your body. It improves your mood by releasing the feel-good chemicals in your brain, including natural endorphins and dopamine! Let Your Angel assist in bringing forth this joyful and healing energy within you.

> **Humor boosts brain function, creativity, memory, and helps you to focus more on problem-solving. I love humor for its creativity factor, and with the guidance of Your Angel, it can help you tap into your innate creative abilities.**

Humor is such a powerful tool for feeling good and improving your overall health and well-being. Your Angel can support you in embracing humor as a daily practice and incorporating it into your life.

> *"I have seen what a laugh can do. It can transform almost unbearable tears into something bearable, even hopeful."* — Bob Hope

Many people are very sensitive these days, and what one finds funny may seem offensive to another. **It's essential to connect with those who have a similar sense of humor as you do and to nurture and expand that sense of humor.** Seek guidance from Your Angel to connect you with like-minded people who can share in the joy and laughter with you. If you don't have anyone in your life with a good sense of humor, then ask Your Angel to join in with you for a good hardy belly laugh about this weird thing called life!

You may not agree, but George Carlin was a master at having a unique perspective of the world and his ability to use humor to challenge conventional thinking and social norms. It's important to keep an open mind and a sense of humor about life, and Your Angel can provide guidance and support in cultivating this mindset.

> *"I think it's the duty of the comedian to find out where the line is drawn and cross it deliberately"*
> *— George Carlin*

Your Angel can help you navigate that line, bringing humor into your life in a way that is authentic and uplifting.

> *"Have you ever noticed that anyone driving slower than you is an idiot, and anyone going faster than you is a maniac?" — George Carlin*

What if you begin to allow yourself to find lightheartedness and humor in everyday situations? Imagine how much easier and happier life would be if you could let go of all of the little stuff that is out of your control anyway.

What's an Angel's favorite dessert? Angel food cake – it's simply heavenly!

I love silly jokes and fun little puns. There are brilliant people who are always coming up with funny sayings and memes. Let humor guide your way, and invite in Your Angel to share the laughter and playfulness with you.

Laugh at yourself instead of getting mad at yourself; a HUGE shift will happen.

What did the Angel say when someone asked for directions to the clouds? "Just wing it!"

Your Angel is there to offer guidance and support as you navigate the twists and turns of life with a lighthearted spirit.

How do Angels communicate? They use "sigh language!"

> "Laughter and tears are both responses to frustration and exhaustion. I myself prefer to laugh since there is less cleaning up to do afterward." — Kurt Vonnegut

This chapter brings to the spotlight the benefits of finding the funny in life. It emphasizes the importance of surrounding yourself with the ability to giggle at shenanigans and to seek guidance from Your Angel to infuse positivity and lightheartedness into your life. Your Angel can help you embrace humor as a daily practice to bring in more joy and fulfillment in your everyday situations.

Let yourself be tickled by all of the monkey business in your life, you will reduce stress, improve your mood, boost your brain function, and tap into your endless creative abilities. Connect with like-minded people who share a similar sense of humor or watch comedians whom you resonate with. Ultimately, remember to be gentle with yourself, learn to laugh at the tomfoolery, and seek the guidance of Your Angel. It's kooky times for sure, so wag more and bark less!

We don't laugh because we feel good, we feel good because we laugh.

— *Bob Ross*

What if... this life was a cosmic comedy show, and I gave myself permission to laugh at all the punchlines? Ha Ha Ha!

Dear Angel of Humor, I find myself filled with frustration and anger over something my loved one has done. I ask for your guidance and assistance in finding the humor of this situation. Please reassure me that this moment is as fleeting as a sitcom punchline. Help me embrace being light hearted like a feather and allow me to let go of the anger and find ease once again. Let me know that having a sense of humor about life will help me swiftly move through difficulties and once again feel good. Let's Ha, Ha, Ha, Ha, Ha, Ha, Ha, Ha, Haaaaaaa Hah Together!!! Thank you, thank you, thank you.

Why did the Angel invest in technology? To have a piece of the cloud.

Creative Practice

Laughter Doodle:

- Write out a minor annoyance in your life, whether it's a one-time or recurring irritation. Express this annoyance through words.

- Then, shift your focus by writing out a cheerful "Ha Ha Ha" around it, joined by doodles that radiate light-heartedness and humor for you.

Transforming a minor annoyance into a playful moment can bring a sense of ease and a broader perspective on the topic. Explore the creative practice as a means to turn frustration into amusement.

Onward, let's embrace ways of letting go of the unknown in order to find something better…

Suffering is not holding you. You are holding suffering. When you become good at the art of letting sufferings go, then you'll come to realize how unnecessary it was for you to drag those burdens around with you. You'll see that no one else other than you was responsible. The truth is that existence wants your life to become a festival.

— *Osho*

Chapter 15

The Wise Farmer

Letting Go Of Expectations And Embracing The Unknown

How can My Angel guide me to embrace the unknown and let go of expectations?

The Wise Farmer

In a small village, there lived a wise old farmer. One day, his only horse ran away. Upon hearing the news, his neighbors came to console him, saying, "What terrible luck! You've lost your horse. How unfortunate!"

The wise farmer calmly replied, "Maybe."

A few days later, the farmer's horse returned, leading a herd of wild horses to the farm. The neighbors were overjoyed and exclaimed, "What incredible luck! Now you have many horses. How fortunate!"

The wise farmer replied, "Maybe."

The following week, while attempting to tame one of the wild horses, the farmer's son fell off and broke his leg. Again, the neighbors came to offer their sympathies, saying, "How unlucky! Your son has been injured. What a terrible turn of events!"

The wise farmer replied, "Maybe."

Soon after, a war broke out in the region, and all able-bodied young men were drafted into the army. The farmer's son, with his broken leg, was exempted from service. The neighbors, realizing the gravity of the situation, said, "How fortunate that your son is not going to war. You are truly blessed!"

The wise farmer, once again, replied, "Maybe."

This story illustrates the principle of letting go and embracing uncertainty. The farmer's ability to let go of rigid judgments and expectations allowed him to navigate life's ups and downs without unnecessary suffering. Instead of clinging to preconceived notions of what is good or bad, he remained open to the possibilities that each situation presented.

Now… I love this story, but I can also be a very reactive person. When bad news strikes, I feel it before my mind can make sense of it all. That said, the emphasis of this story is the mindset of embracing the unknown, accepting the impermanence of life, and letting go of rigid judgments. It encourages you to approach life's circumstances with openness and flexibility, **recognizing that what may initially appear as a setback can sometimes lead to unexpected opportunities.** By cultivating a mindset of letting go, you can find greater peace and resilience in the face of life's ever-changing nature.

Understanding Expectations

Let's explore expectations and how to navigate them.

Expectations are beliefs or hopes about how you think things should or shouldn't happen, how people should or shouldn't behave, or how situations should or shouldn't unfold.

They can range from small daily expectations to grandiose hopes for the future. However, when your expectations are not met, you often experience disappointment, frustration, or even devastation. It is important to examine why you hold these expectations and how they impact your emotional state.

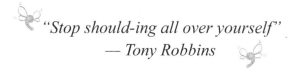

"Stop should-ing all over yourself"
— *Tony Robbins*

Don't Throw The Baby Out With The Bathwater

You've heard people say, "Don't Throw the baby out with the bathwater," this illustrates the tendency to focus on eliminating something harmful or undesirable while inadvertently disregarding something valuable in the process.

One classic scene fitting to this example can be found in the movie "The Pink Panther" (2006), directed by Shawn Levy. In this comedy film, Inspector Jacques Clouseau, played by Steve Martin, is a bumbling and inept detective assigned to solve the murder of a famous soccer coach and find the stolen Pink Panther diamond.

In one particular scene, Clouseau is searching for a clue that he believes is hidden inside a large antique safe. Determined to retrieve the clue, he proceeds to use various methods, including explosives and a chainsaw, to open the safe. However, his attempts go disastrously wrong, and the entire room begins to crumble and collapse around him. Furniture, walls, and even the ceiling come crashing down, creating chaos, destruction, and havoc.

As the scene progresses, Clouseau's determination to retrieve the clue leads to a series of escalating destructive actions, resulting in the complete destruction of the room. Despite the excessive and unnecessary destruction, Clouseau remains oblivious to the chaos he has caused exemplifying the concept of "throwing the baby out with the bathwater" in a comical and exaggerated manner, as Clouseau's single-minded pursuit of the clue leads to the total destruction of the entire room.

So, if you stub your toe first thing in the morning, try to stop instead of becoming so fixated on the discomfort that you overlook the potential for a good day. Slowing down and reflecting on what is going on can help prevent further injury or a Clouseau catastrophe day!

Action vs. Acceptance

There is a distinction between having expectations and taking action towards what you desire.

> **Change doesn't happen by complaining about a situation; it happens through problem-solving and deciding on the best course of action.**

Some circumstances call for our proactive efforts, while others require acceptance of what is. It is essential to discern when to act and when to practice acceptance, understanding that you can only control your response to situations, not the actions of others.

The Power Of: Or Something Better...

In your quest for specific outcomes, you often cling tightly to your expectations. However, incorporating the phrase **"or something better" opens you up to possibilities beyond what you can currently envision or desire.** This allows for the potential of an even greater outcome than you can currently imagine for yourself.

By letting go of your attachment to specific outcomes and trusting in the guidance of Your Angel, you allow room for unexpected blessings and opportunities to manifest. This mindset fosters optimism, hope, and adaptability.

Navigating Expectations

To navigate expectations, here is a reflective practice to help guide you toward letting go of the suffering and instead begin to step into action.

- **Assess The Situation:** Evaluate the situation with a beginner's mind and determine if there is something you can do to address it. Take into account whether it is within your influence or not.

- **Action Steps:** If there is an actionable step you can take, identify the specific actions you can initiate to bring about the desired change. This proactive approach empowers you to make a positive step forward.

- **Letting Go:** If the situation is beyond your control or there is nothing you can do at the moment, it may be necessary to let it go. Reflect on what you need to release or surrender to find peace and acceptance in the moment. This step enables you to reduce unnecessary suffering and cultivate resilience.

- **Future Considerations:** Recognize that some situations may require time, space, or reevaluation in the future. Consider whether the issue at hand needs further attention at a later date. This allows for flexibility and acknowledges that circumstances can evolve. Maneuvering expectations asks you to be self-aware, flexible, and willing to embrace the unknown. By understanding the impact of expectations, practicing acceptance, and taking inspired action when necessary, you can find a balance between your desires and what is out of your control.

→ **Mirroring:** The idea of "mirroring" suggests that you often notice in others the qualities or behaviors that you either strongly desire or strongly dislike in yourself. It's like a reflection of your own wishes or challenges. For instance, if someone's confidence impresses you, it might indicate that you secretly wish for more self-assurance. On the flip side, if someone's impatience annoys you, it could be a trait you're not comfortable admitting you also possess. This concept reminds you to look at your reactions to others as a way to learn about yourself and the things you might need to work on or embrace within yourself.

By letting go and staying open to possibilities, you allow Your Angel to unfold its magic, bringing forth outcomes that may surpass your expectations. The journey is just as important as the destination, and embracing the unknown can lead to remarkable expansion and fulfillment in your life.

In conclusion, continue to ask Your Angel for help and guidance on this journey and start adding in what you want… or something better.

"The truth will set you free, but first it will piss you off." — Gloria Steinem

This chapter explores the importance of letting go of expectations and embracing the unknown. Remember Osho's quote, emphasizing that "suffering is not inherent to us but rather something we hold onto". By adopting a mindset of openness and flexibility, illustrated by the story of the wise farmer, you can move through life's ups and downs without unnecessary suffering. This chapter provides insights on understanding expectations, distinguishing between action and acceptance, incorporating the phrase "or something better," and navigating expectations through self-awareness and flexibility. By letting go of rigid judgments and embracing the possibilities that each situation presents, you can experience more expansion, peace, and resilience in your life.

What if... I started to let go of expectations and instead open up to all of the possibilities?

Dear Angel of the Unknown, please help me let go of my expectations of how other people should or shouldn't act. Please release any suffering I've allowed given their words and actions. I ask that you guide me to letting go of what others do and instead focus on what I can do better and what I want to accomplish... OR SOMETHING BETTER! Thank you, thank you, thank you!

Creative Practice

Letting Go Doodle:

- 💜 Take a moment to express, either with words or doodles, something that you wish to release from your life— a habit, an action, or a thought that lingers in your mind that no longer serves your well-being.

- 💜 Imagine what would happen if you were able to let it go, and express the emotions and sensations associated with releasing this from your life. What would life look like and feel like without this burden?

- 💜 Allow your creative exploration to guide you and allow Your Angel to be there with you.

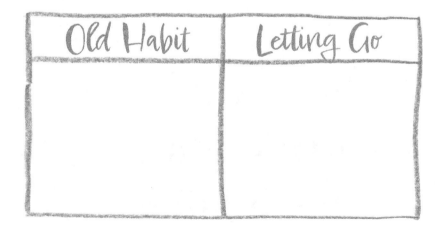

Moving right along into the next chapter, let's discover what new beginnings are available for you…

Embrace uncertainty. Some of the most beautiful chapters in our lives won't have a title until much later.

— *Bob Goff*

Chapter 16
Metamorphosis

Embracing Change And Transformation

How can I embrace uncertainty and open myself up to new beginnings?

Metamorphosis

Once, there was a caterpillar who believed her destiny was to crawl on the ground. One day, she noticed a beautiful butterfly and was captivated by her freedom. The caterpillar yearned for the same liberation and approached the butterfly to ask her for guidance.

The butterfly shared her own transformational story, explaining that she, too, had once been a caterpillar. She realized her potential for more and embraced the discomfort of growth. Shedding limiting beliefs, she surrendered to the transformative process.

Inspired, the caterpillar set off on a journey of self-discovery. She challenged her beliefs, embraced change, and eventually spun a chrysalis—a hard, protective outer shell or cocoon. Inside the chrysalis, the insect's tissues and organs broke down and reorganized to form the adult insect, a process known as metamorphosis. Inside, she dissolved her old self and underwent a profound transformation.

Emerging as a magnificent butterfly, she soared through the open skies, embracing the freedom and endless possibilities that awaited her. The caterpillar had broken free from her limitations, opening herself to a world of new opportunities.

This story reminds you that by challenging your beliefs and embracing change, you can transform yourself and discover the boundless potential within you.

> **Like the caterpillar, you have the power to break free from the constraints of your past and embrace a future filled with growth, freedom, and possibility.**

Transformation

I've witnessed this transformation in my hypnotherapy clients. One of the most heartwarming stories involves a client who had convinced herself that she was incapable of maintaining a successful relationship, believing that she always found a way to sabotage it. During the 'investigation' phase of the hypnotherapy session where I'm asking questions and she's able to look into her subconscious to find the answers, we unearthed a significant childhood memory. At a young age, she had observed her parents constantly arguing and fighting. In her young mind, she looked up to her parents and made a profound decision: if this was what relationships and marriage looked like, she wanted no part of it.

> **As we connected this childhood experience to her current struggles with the desire to form healthy and loving relationships, a lightning bolt of realization struck her. She understood that she had made this decision at such a tender young age, concluding that love and marriage were synonymous with hardship, fear, and pain—something she didn't want!**

Her breakthrough was remarkable. The following day, she shared a small but meaningful success. A neighbor had kindly offered to help her with some yard work. Instead of her usual response of 'No, that's okay, I can handle it,' she simply said 'okay' and accepted the kind gesture. This small shift marked the beginning of a profound change. She recognized the connection between her past experiences, her old habit of pushing people away, and this one small act of embracing change. And from there, her life got better and more connected.

Being open to what the future holds will help you move past limiting beliefs. If you want something but don't believe you can achieve it, you can ask Your Angel, "What are my limiting beliefs that prevent me from believing that I can do it?" Can you open yourself up again to that dream? Can you live more fully and remember to ask Your Angel to help you achieve what you want?

Your Angel, in turn, asks you to believe in yourself when you seek their assistance. It's a give-and-take. Can you open your mind, heart, and soul to the fact that you can go through life filling it with passion, purpose, and fulfillment?

Do you try to piece together and understand the meaning and significance of your life? Do you question the things that are constantly controlling the scripts within your subconscious mind, influencing your decisions and patterns of thinking?

> **Do you realize that everyone, including you, is "programmed" from a very young age with beliefs?**

Have you ever wondered about people who have overcome horrific events? James Allen, the author of "As a Man Thinketh," wrote his book after surviving the Holocaust. His words resonate: "As he thinks, so he is and he continues to think, so he remains."

How is it that a person coming from immense difficulties can succeed while others, seemingly with less trauma, fall into the depths of addiction and despair? It all comes down to your **belief systems.**

I grew up with some "fun" (sarcasm) sayings —

- "Children are to be seen and not heard."
- "I brought you into this world and I can take you out."
- "Only lucky people get to do what they love."
- and "If you are fat, no man will want you."

Oh, and there was a **scroll** on the kitchen wall that read "Insanity is hereditary, you get it from your kids."

I've had to dismantle those hypnotic messages to create my own empowering life slogans so that I could stop being a victim, stop believing that crap, and be my own person. My parents, bless their hearts, didn't know better, it is what was done to them. These stories have become ingrained within our psyche, repeated to ourselves over and over again. Often they become as unconscious as the habit of eating every day.

> **You, too, have a story and a narrative that's holding you back and disempowering you.**

Interrupting The Hypnotic State

> **Are you ready to interrupt this hypnotic state?**

Assuming that's a Yes? Great… let's jump into some easy ways to get started.

It may sound silly, but I challenge you to start using your least dominant hand for simple activities that you do hypnotically every day such as brushing your teeth, writing, and eating.

For some who are ambidextrous, this may be easy, and for some who have a dominant hand, this may be a bit more challenging… and that's a good thing.

Have you ever driven home, a drive that you've done hundreds of times, just to arrive at home and have no recollection of the drive … guess what…you were in a hypnotic state.

But if something unusual happens during that hypnotic state, you quickly wake up…

> **By doing something different, you snap yourself out of habitual patterns and negative hypnotic states that you wish to break free from.**

Using your non-dominant hand helps to activate the opposite side of your brain which can lead to increased creativity and problem-solving abilities. It can help you develop patience and perseverance because you have to approach things as a beginner. It can help you break habitual patterns of movement and behavior that you want to change. You can improve your fine motor skills by drawing, writing, and brushing your teeth with your non-dominant hand. This also improves eye-hand coordination.

Using your non-dominant hand helps you become awake and aware of everyday things that are all too often set on auto-pilot. Being more present and aware is the best way to truly notice little wonderful things throughout your day. It's as if Your Angel is sharing everyday things with you in a new way. You can also look at this as another form of Moving Meditation.

It can be challenging and uncomfortable at first, but with practice, it will become easier and more natural. This will help you connect both sides of your brain, and help you become more present and aware of your daily doings.

Let's dispel the myth of multitasking—an illusion that distracts you from being present and fully engaged in what you are trying to accomplish. The more immersed you become in the present moment, the less you succumb to habitual or hypnotic thought patterns, actions, and accidents.

Utilizing this powerful tool, you can continue on the path of intentional change, cultivating new empowering habits while shedding those that no longer serve you. By embracing these practices of presence and awareness in everyday activities, you wake yourself up from feeling disconnected, on auto-pilot and wondering where the day went.

Sometimes I paint with my least dominant hand because it's then when I come back to my dominant hand, it's easier than it was before. It's a practice… give it a try!

Embracing change requires you to venture into unfamiliar territory, much like using your non-dominant hand for daily tasks. Initially, it may feel strange, yet as you persist, you begin to notice the intricacies of your actions that you may have previously overlooked. This mirrors the process of rewriting your old stories.

Although there is a natural inclination to return to your familiar narratives—the "dominant hand"—you must strive to embrace change and recognize that the true essence of your being resides beyond those self-imposed limitations. Let Your Angel be your constant companion, cheering you on and celebrating your progress with you, no matter how small.

This is what it feels like to change those old stories. You want to go back to the dominant hand (the old stories) because they seem comfortable and familiar. Ask Your Angel to help you shift and become comfortable with something new and uncomfortable! Let Your Angel be there smiling with you, laughing with you as you stumble through that old courtyard into the place where you really want to be… home… that inner home.

"Sometimes letting go is simply changing the labels you place on an event. Looking at the same event with fresh eyes." — Steve Maraboli

METAMORPHOSIS

In this chapter, the story of the caterpillar's transformation into a beautiful butterfly is shared as a metaphor for transformation and embracing change in your life. This chapter emphasizes the importance of challenging limiting beliefs and being open to new possibilities. It encourages you to interrupt your habitual patterns and negative thought processes by engaging in activities with your non-dominant hand. By doing so, you can increase your creativity, and problem-solving abilities, and become more present and aware in each moment. Also, allow yourself to rewrite old stories and embrace change.

In the beginning quote by Bob Goff, "Embrace uncertainty. Some of the most beautiful chapters in our lives won't have a title until much later." This emphasizes that by embracing change and venturing into unfamiliar territory, you can unlock new opportunities and create new beautiful chapters into your life that you may have never even thought possible for you.

What if... I open up and let the butterfly within me emerge, let go of the stuff that no longer serves me, and in doing so, embrace the endless possibilities that life has in store for me.

Dear Angel of New Beginnings, let me be open to the transformative changes of my life. Let me let go of judgments and fears and embrace the unknown, like a road trip I'm eager to take... or something better! Thank you, thank you, thank you.

Creative Practice

Non-Dominant Hand Doodles:

- Engage in this playful practice by first writing your name with your dominant hand, noticing the confidence you write with.

- Then, switch to your non-dominant hand, and embrace the quirks, loops, and unexpected patterns that emerge as you write your name.

- Pay attention to the unique sensations and experiences that you feel as you fumble through the unfamiliar territory of using your non-dominant hand… thus allowing it to become more familiar.

- Smile, stay curious, and enjoy the newness of this exercise.

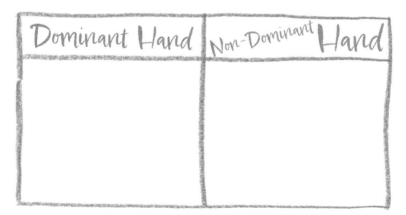

In the pages to come, you'll understand how to better control your emotions…

Your outer journey may contain a million steps; your inner journey only has one: the step you are taking right now.

— *Eckhart Tolle*

Chapter 17

The Alchemist

Response-Ability And Reframing Negative Thoughts

How can I take control of my response to life's ups and downs?

The Alchemist

"The Alchemist" by Paulo Coelho is a captivating tale that beautifully embodies the power of looking within yourself and the transformative nature of consciously choosing how to respond to life's challenges. The butterfly shared her own transformational story, explaining that she, too, had once been a caterpillar. She realized her potential for more and embraced the discomfort of growth. Shedding limiting beliefs, she surrendered to the transformative process.

The story follows the journey of Santiago, a young shepherd in search of his Personal Legend. "When you want something, all the universe conspires to help you achieve it." Along his quest, Santiago encounters setbacks and learns profound lessons about self-discovery. "Don't let others choose your path for you."

As Santiago travels, he realizes that his thoughts and perceptions shape his reality. He understands the importance of looking within, tapping into his inner wisdom, and questioning his beliefs and fears. This looking within enables him to find the courage to pursue his dreams and embrace the unknown. "There is only one thing that makes a dream impossible to achieve: the fear of failure."

"Don't believe the world's greatest lie," warns The Alchemist – "That at a certain point, you lose control and become controlled by fate." Santiago's realization that he can change his mindset and approach to challenges reflects the theme of personal growth and taking responsibility. By looking within and responding more positively, you can transform your life and shape your reality.

Santiago also learns to embrace the present, focus on the process rather than the result, and take risks despite the fear of failure. "When someone makes a decision, he is really diving into a strong current that will carry him to places he has never dreamed of when he first made the decision," **It emphasizes that decisions lead to action, action leads to experience, and experience leads to learning.** Through these teachings, **Paulo Coelho reminds us that making ourselves better contributes to making the world better, and dreams are the possibility that makes life interesting.** Practicing gratitude and staying passionate are key elements in recognizing the good things that happen every day. So, keep dreaming, stay present, cultivate gratitude, follow your heart, and sculpt your own destiny.

This quote helps to sum up my takeaway from The Alchemist, which is **"When you make yourself better, you make the world better."** This inspires me to go for my dreams, stay on my path, be willing to risk failure in order to taste its success and to be more grateful and in the present. When I do this, I then have the energy and ability to help more people, therefore making the world around me a better place.

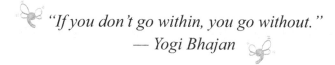

"If you don't go within, you go without."
— Yogi Bhajan

Response-Ability

> **I discovered that by looking WITHIN, looking at MYSELF, and asking to change the way I RESPOND. I created a greater sense of peace and confidence in my ability to better handle situations around me. Therefore, it allows me to move into the SOLUTION and away from the problem.**

Jack Canfield asks us, "What is responsibility?" It is your "ability to respond" or response-ability. What is your ability to respond to the different situations in your life?

How can you control your response? One way is by asking Your Angel for the response that you want.

If you always blow up in anger at someone when you are triggered by something, ask Your Angel to help you respond in the way you want to, in a calmer way.

Example:

A mother might say… Angel, I get so frustrated and then yell at my child when he doesn't clean up after himself. Please help me see that he is a child. His intentions are not bad, so please give me the patience to focus on what is good about him. Let me see if there is another approach I can take that helps instill the importance of cleaning but doesn't lead to aggravation or strain on our relationship… or something better. Thank you, thank you, thank you!

> *"You must take personal responsibility. You cannot change the circumstances, the seasons or the wind, but you can change yourself. That is something you have charge of." — Jim Rohn*

Allowing yourself to be response-able, meaning able to respond in the way you do want. This gives you control over the way you think and feel. You only have control of one thing, and that's your thinking, and when you can control your thinking, you have much more control over responses and actions in your life.

Ways To Become Response-Able

Practice self-awareness, write down the thoughts that you have going on in your head all the time, look at them, and see which ones are positive and which ones are negative.

For the negative thoughts write them down on the left side of the paper, and then on the right side reframe it, and write down a more positive antidote to the negative thought.

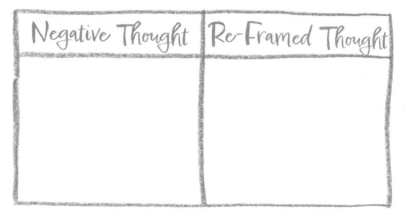

When the negative thoughts pop up (and it will), remind yourself of the re-framed positive one as soon as you become aware of the negative thought. Keep on this and you'll be amazed at how this will become easier and easier to catch and release.

> **This may feel awkward and difficult at first, so start with just one negative thought reframed into a positive one. Once you have accomplished switching one thought, this will give you the confidence and empowerment to continue doing this with the next and next thought that needs to be reframed.**

If you start with all of them, you might find yourself spending all day doing this, and too much too fast can lead to a quick burnout. Little by little… baby step by baby step.

> *"Habit is habit and not to be flung out the window by any man, but coaxed downstairs one step at a time."* — Mark Twain

If it's too big, it's overwhelming and can create procrastination. By breaking it down into smaller steps, little by little it's more manageable and it will reduce the stress and anxiety of the "bigness" of the topic and help you make progress on your goal.

Small Steps = Strong Habits

Using Continuous Small Steps Will Help These Habits Truly Stick! It's better to go for a five-minute walk every day and slowly increase the habit of getting out for a walk. This will create the habit much quicker than trying to walk for one hour every day and finding that you keep putting it off.

Think about the gym, if you don't already go to the gym but you've signed up for that one New Year's resolution to go to the gym… do you go once? Work out too hard? Then can't return the next day because you are sore? Sound familiar?

I know, I know… Nicole, you keep repeating this. I know, that's because it often seems so simple that it's worth repeating so that you don't glaze over it and therefore not give it a try.

It's truly better to start small. I know all of the self-help gurus out there tell you to "just do it" but if you have been round and round this merry-go-round before… let's stop the insanity and try something new. Starting small means much more progress than going fast and burning out even quicker, or not starting at all because it seems way too overwhelming.

As mentioned in previous chapters, reframing your negative thoughts IS MOST EFFECTIVE when you write down the negative thought and THEN write down the more positive thought next to it.

EXAMPLE: Gosh I'm so stupid.

CHANGE TO:
- **I can do this - slow down and be patient, I can figure this out.**

- Then take a deep breath, think of the one next step to take, and do your best to take just that one little step.

- Take a deep breath and become present in what you are doing and what you want to accomplish.

Positive affirmations can be tricky! Because your mind has to believe it first!

- If your mind says - I'll never be able to do this - change your language and remember the power of YET.

- I'm not able to do this…YET… but I want to, so the small steps I'm willing to take are _____

- And then break it down into one little step that you know you can accomplish quickly and easily.

Take Action

"A journey of a thousand miles begins with a single step." — Lao Tzu

It's time to STOP the OLD negative thought and RE-FRAME it with a more pro-active, positive, and ENCOURAGING thought. It has to be something that your brain will BELIEVE or is said in a way that your mind will accept.

Your emotional well-being will skyrocket when you catch and reframe the negative and harsh things you say to yourself throughout the day.

"The old saying goes, "Sticks and stones may break my bones, but words will never hurt me." Yet, my own negative self-talk is certain to make my words both sticks and stones."
— Craig D. Lounsbrough

The focus of this chapter is on your inner journey and the power of looking within yourself. Paulo Coelho's transformative story and wisdom of The Alchemist sums it up with… "When you want something, all the universe conspires in helping you achieve it." We explored the transformative nature of self-reflection, conscious choice, and personal responsibility. It highlights the importance of practicing self-awareness, reframing negative thoughts, taking small steps, and using positive and believable affirmations to shape your thinking to respond the way you want to when you are presented with life's challenges. Begin or continue your inner journey, and ask Your Angel for help whenever you need, want, or feel stuck in any way. Remember…

When you make yourself better, you make the world better.

— Paulo Coelho

What if... I take just one step, or just one positive thought towards my true journey? What if I would allow myself to write it down and engage with it?

Dear Angel of Responsiveness, let me see my actions as a reflection in the mirror. Guide me to make the necessary changes within myself and to become the better person I truly wish to be - connected, authentic, wise, creative, grounded, and fulfilled... or something even better! Thank you, thank you, thank you.

Creative Practice

Inner Journey Doodle:

- 💜 Grab pen and paper, and begin to doodle or draw out words that capture the spirit of the journey you wish to travel upon.

- 💜 Invite in the presence of Your Angel as your creative companion, seeking assistance whenever you encounter a crossroad.

- 💜 Let this visual exploration be a vibrant reflection of the inner odyssey you aspire for.

- 💜 Dive into the Creative Practice, and let Your Angel's guidance infuse your artistic expression.

Ask Journey Alchemist Adventure Believe Inner Journey My Response Small Steps Dream

Next, let's open up more ways to easily communicate with Your Angel…

www.NicoleWhiteWellness.com

You can have anything you want if you are willing to give up the belief that you can't have it.

— *Dr. Robert Anthony*

Chapter 18
The Lady In White

Belief Like A Child

How can I be open to the idea that it's possible to communicate with My Angel?

Lady In White

My friend Paul told me many times about a "Lady In White" who would visit him as a child. He thought that she was a spirit like an older sister or a younger aunt. She taught him how to fix things and how to ride a bike. He told his mother about this "Lady In White," and at first, she thought he had an imaginary friend. She also found it funny and cute. However, as time went on, she became curious and a little spooked by his encounters. He would be heard talking to the "Lady In White" in his room.

Paul recalls getting a bike for his sixth birthday. It was an old banana seat Schwinn-style bike with big handlebars. It was pretty big for him, so he looked really small on it. It was difficult for him to ride since he transitioned from a small bike with training wheels to a full-sized bike.

On the day of his birthday, his aunt and uncle tried to teach him how to ride the bike. He was having problems and kept falling over. He persisted, even when it was time for dinner. Paul told his family that he didn't want to eat; he wanted to keep trying to ride his new bike.

Just as they were finishing up dinner, Paul ran inside and excitedly told them that he could ride his bike! They were skeptical since he hadn't been doing well before dinner, and only less than an hour had passed since they were last outside with him.

Paul said, They all came outside, and I got on my bike and rode off down the sidewalk. As I started down the sidewalk, I turned my head and said, "You can let go now." I rode down the sidewalk, turned the bike around, and rode back to our house. When I got back, my mom asked, "Who were you talking to when you said to let go?" I told her that "the Lady in White was teaching me how to ride my bike while you were eating dinner. She was running alongside me and holding the bike steady as I started out down the sidewalk until I got my balance."

Paul moved from that home not long after that. As an adult, he tries to dismiss it, no longer believing in the Lady In White (Angel). Nevertheless, it was clear that as a child, this friend, this companion, this loving being was there for him and spoke to him because he was open to it.

"Some things have to be believed to be seen."
— Madeleine L'Engle

Now, I have never had an experience like Paul, but when he told me this story, I felt it, I believed him, and I longed for that kind of connection with a "spirit," with An Angel!

Creating Belief

What if the best way to communicate with Your Angel is to be open to the idea that it's possible?

What if you don't have to see the Angel or have an experience like Paul?

What if you could create in your mind and believe with your whole being that Your Angel is truly there for you?

You could call it a Guardian Angel, Your Angel, an Arch-Angel, or even a very specific Angel with a singular task, such as the Angel of Writing, the Angel of Food, the Angel of Air, the Angel of Health, or the Angel of Good Feelings.

> **People have believed in Angels for thousands of years, so why not you and me?**

How To Communicate With Your Angel

I encourage you to embrace what resonates with you about the Angels and incorporate them into your life. Some people have shared their beliefs about the Angels—what they are or aren't, what they do or don't do. However, I want to share something truly transformative with you.

Think about a child, whether it's you as a child, a child you know, or a child you've heard of, who has a "special friend." Some adults may call it an "imaginary friend," but to that child, if given the chance to speak openly and without judgment about this "being," they would tell you all sorts of stories about it, and they believe it is as real as you or me.

> *"To be unafraid of the judgment of others is the greatest freedom you can have."*
> *— Timothy Shriver*

Practice Finding Your Angel

Deepening your connection to Your Angel is a practice. Just like anything else you want to incorporate into your life, you have to practice, practice, practice. Here are just a few ways you can begin that practice.

- **Asking:** Request guidance and support from Your Angel. Some may call this prayer. It can help you feel more connected, and the stronger the connection, the more you'll receive their messages.

- **Writing:** Putting your thoughts, feelings, and experiences in writing can help you become more receptive to the guidance Your Angel is providing.

- **Signs & Symbols:** Many believe that Angels communicate with us through signs and symbols such as coins, feathers, butterflies, coincidences, or repeated number sequences also known as Angel numbers. Paying attention to these signs and trusting your intuition can open you up to more messages from Your Angel.

- **Meditation:** Find a comfortable place to sit and focus on your breath. By quieting your mind, you open yourself up to receiving messages from Your Angel.

Communicating with Your Angel is personal, and everyone's experience will be different. Your connection to Your Angel is special and will depend on your beliefs, practices, and experiences.

Stay open to how you receive messages and explore different ways to connect with Your Angel.

Take care and enjoy the journey!

 "Sometimes, the signs from Angels can be subtle, but if you keep an open mind and heart, you will be able to recognize them."
— *Laura Lynne Jackson*

This chapter invites you into the idea of believing or beginning to believe in the ability to connect with Your Angel. It recounts the story of a friend who had encounters with a "Lady in White" (Angel) as a child, highlighting the power of natural belief and openness of a beginner's mind. We explored practical tips for deepening your connection with Your Angel, such as still and moving meditations, asking for guidance, writing, and paying attention to signs and symbols. It encourages you to embrace your own beliefs and to give the Creative Practices a test drive to explore and allow yourself to encounter signs from Your Angel.

What if... just for today, I started to believe in **My Angel** and was open to the signs she gives me? (Finding coins, feathers, repeated number sequences when looking at the clock, a butterfly, coincidences, serendipities, etc.)

Dear Angel of Communication, take away all of this doubt that keeps me from truly believing. Let me believe in you as a child would believe. Let your very being nourish me, just as a large glass of water would hydrate me when thirsty, or something better! Thank you, thank you, thank you.

Creative Practice

Symbolic Serendipities Doodle:

- Grab some paper and pen, and think about some symbols and serendipities you've experienced.

- Begin to write, draw, and doodle about encounters you've had or aspire to have with Your Angel — be it butterflies, coins, feathers, or anything else that sparks a sense of magic.

- Let your imagination run wild as you capture symbols or serendipities of your connection with Your Angel.

- Dive into this creative practice and explore the whimsical world of signs from Your Angel.

As you turn the page, let's find out what your unique creativity looks like…

Art is something that lies in the soul of a human being, and one cannot measure it by an external yardstick.

— *Nick Bantock*

Chapter 19
ISH

Creative Practice Part II

How can I fully embrace my own unique creativity and use it to help me navigate through life?

ISH

Another "book I love by Peter H. Reynolds is "Ish."

The story of "Ish" revolves around a young boy named Ramon, who loves to draw.

One day, Ramon's older brother Leon looks over at one of Ramon's drawings of a vase, and criticizes it, saying that it doesn't look like a real vase. This deeply upsets Ramon and makes him doubt his artistic abilities. He starts to believe that he can't draw.

Feeling discouraged, Ramon begins drawing with self-critical thoughts instead of the excited and creative enthusiasm he used to draw with. He becomes fixated on creating perfect drawings, but he can't seem to achieve his ideal. He then crumples up each drawing with frustration when he can't reach the perfection that he wants.

Then one day, his little sister, Marisol, grabs one of his crumpled-up drawings and runs into her room. Ramon runs after her and discovers his crumpled drawings up on Marisol's walls, and realizes that she has treasured them for their unique qualities. She tells him that his drawings are "ish," meaning they are not perfect replicas but still capture the essence of what he was drawing.

Inspired by Marisol's perspective, Ramon shifts his mindset, opens up, embraces the idea of "ish" and begins to draw again, letting go of his self-imposed standards of perfection. He learns to appreciate the beauty of Ish-drawing… and discovers the joy of expressing himself through his art without worrying about meeting unrealistic expectations.

The story of "Ish" encourages you to embrace your creativity and find the beauty in your unique artistic expressions, even if they don't conform to traditional standards of creativity. It celebrates the freedom of self-expression and the importance of valuing your own creative voice.

I share this story in my You CAN Paint! 5-Day Challenges and ongoing course. I love it when community members share a painting with the group and call it an ISH drawing. They will say it's Tree-Ish, Bird-Ish, Cloud-Ish, and so forth.

Using The Creative Practice
Part II

It can be a tough world when you feel alone or lost in it, but it doesn't have to be that way. By embracing the Creative Practices that resonate with you, it gives you an outlet, a friend, someone to call on: Your Angel!

> *"You just call out my name*
> *And you know, wherever I am*
> *I'll come runnin'*
> *To see you again*
> *Winter, spring, summer or fall*
> *All you have to do is call*
> *And I'll be there*
> *You've got a friend"*
> *— Song by Carole King*

Your Angel will help you feel that you always have someone to turn to, whether you need to go inward or take action for safety, help, guidance, or love.

Since you were born as a creative being (we are all born creatives), you can use any of the Creative Practices and begin to use these tools to write, draw, paint, sew, cook, sing, dance, or engage in any Creative Practice to help you through even the most difficult of times and events.

The creative practice is anything positive, productive, or healing that works for you.

"I'm not very creative" doesn't work. There's no such thing as creative people and non-creative people. There are only people who use their creativity and people who don't.

> *Unused creativity doesn't just disappear. It lives within us until it's expressed, neglected to death, or suffocated by resentment and fear."*
> *— Brené Brown*

Just Some Of The Creative Practices

- **Breathing Exercises:** Take a deep breath in and let it out slowly. This simple act can release stress, anxiety, and worry. Smokers often turn to smoking as a way to take deep breaths, but you can develop a healthier habit of going outside and taking deep breaths with Your Angel.

- **Cleaning:** Imagine you are with her, singing and "chopping wood and carrying water," allowing it to cleanse your spirit and create a more energetic space.

- **Cooking:** Cooking is a creative activity because it involves using a variety of ingredients to create flavors and textures in food. The cooking itself and presentation are creative acts as well. If you love cooking, you can create your own cookbook by compiling your favorite recipes into a book. I also love to play with my food and make faces or shapes out of them just to be silly. It's also healthier to cook your own food and make it with love. Your Angel will be with you, helping you put love and care into the food you are preparing.

- **Drawing or Doodling:** Draw out Your Angel. Drawing, sketching, and doodling are all fantastic ways to get into your creative brain and connect with Your Angel. Remember the insights from "The Dot" and "ISH", start with an ISH drawing, and carry a sketchbook with you to capture little moments in time. Bring Your Angel with you, let her draw and doodle with you.

- **Gardening:** Gardening is creating living artwork. You get to choose from different plants, flowers, and trees to create a beautiful healing space. Gardening involves being surrounded by color and texture. If I had a garden, I think it would have An Angel for each plant, fruit, vegetable, tree, and flower. Gardening is natural exercise, stress relief, and improves mental health because of all the benefits of being outside and in nature. It also reminds me of the joy of Garden Fairies. There are amazing pictures you can find online of people who create elaborate and amazing fairy gardens... aka Angels.

- **Humor:** Laugh with Your Angel. Find the humor in life. Look around and ask yourself, what's funny about this situation?

- **Movement:** Bring Your Angel in, let her move with you. Ask Your Angel for the strength, flexibility, and endurance that you want, and imagine her walking, dancing, and exercising along with you.

- **Nature:** Imagine Your Angel being in nature with you. Angels love so many places in this world, from the ocean to the mountains to the forests to little parks in the neighborhood, to a plant in your house, porch, or yard.

- **Painting & Mixed Media:** Paint Your Angel, and let her guide you in your creativity. There are numerous ways that painting and mixed media are helpful and healing. If you are interested in learning more, just check our You CAN Paint! Creative Community at www.NicoleWhiteWellness.com

- **Pets:** If you have pets and love them, talk to them as you would An Angel—for they are closer to one than you think.

- **Photography:** Photography is creative expression captured. What do you love to photograph? Photograph things that make you feel amazing in this world, perhaps a place where the Angels might be hanging out unseen.

- **Fiber Arts - Knitting, crochet, needlepoint, etc.:** Put the essence of Your Angel into your pieces. What are the colors, the textures, the patterns... bring her into your world.

- **Singing:** Sing with and to Your Angel. Singing reduces stress and anxiety. Think about what happens when your favorite song comes on and you sing along with it... Happy! Music is very powerful, and just like your thoughts, it's important to understand what you are letting into your mind. Listen to angry music... you might feel angry. Listen to sad music... you will probably start to feel sad. Listen to upbeat music with fun lyrics... you get the point. I have a feeling that Your Angel really loves it when you sing. It's not what you sound like, it's the intention and childlike abandonment within it that they love and adore.

> *"Here's a little song I wrote*
> *You might want to sing it note for note*
> *Don't worry, be happy*
> *In every life we have some trouble*
> *But when you worry, you make it double*
> *Don't worry, be happy*
> *Don't worry, be happy now"*
> *— Song by Bobbie McFerrin*

- **Travel & Adventure:** Bring Your Angel with you on your adventures. See them in the new amazing places you experience, bring them along, talk to them, thank them, and appreciate the beauty of this world with Your Angel.

- **Writing:** Write to Your Angel and imagine that Your Angel is writing back. I love doing this; it's a great practice and I always find some pretty remarkable things that are written. Writing is so powerful, more on that in the next chapter.

Incomplete List Of Possibilities For Your Creative Practice

- Acting
- Animation
- Calligraphy
- Candle Making
- Ceramics
- Collage
- Comedy
- Cooking
- Creative Journaling
- Creative Visualization
- Crochet
- Dancing
- Digital Art
- Drawing
- Film Making
- Game Design
- Gardening
- Graphic Design
- Improvisation
- Knitting
- Leathercraft
- Meditative Practice
- Metalworking
- Mindfulness
- Origami
- Painting
- Paper Mache
- Photography
- Playing Instruments
- Pottery
- Printmaking
- Quilting
- Rock Painting
- Scrapbooking
- Sculpture
- Sewing
- Singing
- Stained Glass Art
- Storytelling
- Textile Arts
- Tie-Dye
- Travel Sketching
- Upcycling
- Urban Sketching
- Videography
- Virtual Reality Art
- Web Design
- Woodworking
- Writing (Creative Writing, Poetry, Fiction, Non-fiction)

I use these Creative Practices in my time of frustration, loneliness, and need. I use this for clarity, for peace, and to help myself understand this world. I use these practices to relieve depression, anxiety, and feelings of helplessness and hopelessness when horrible things are happening in this world.

I also use these Creative Practices when I'm happy and feel alive and wanting to capture the world through drawing or writing. I bring My Angel along with me to enjoy the sweetness of this life. You get to take Your Angel with you anywhere you go! Happy or sad, they always love to be with you!

This is not a conditional relationship where you can only ask them for help when you feel good or feel you have something to give in return. **You can ask for help at any time!**

The benefits are out of this world when it comes to engaging in creativity. There are so many Creative Practices available for you. We are all artists. You, too, were once a child who could easily pick up a crayon and make meaningful marks. If you don't remember or you stopped really early, I'm guessing someone said something to make you compare yourself or doubt your creative abilities, and I'm really sorry you had to experience that. The best way to fix that part of the past, if that happened to you, is to empower yourself to pick up any of the Creative Practices that interest you. Allow yourself to be a beginner again and to fill yourself with wonder and Curiosità :).

 "Creativity itself doesn't care at all about results – the only thing it craves is the process. Learn to love the process and let whatever happens next happen, without fussing too much about it. Work like a monk, or a mule, or some other representative metaphor for diligence. Love the work. Destiny will do what it wants with you, regardless." — Elizabeth Gilbert

This chapter wants to instill in you that you have the vast potential for creativity as your birthright. It highlights the subjective and personal nature of art. This is meant to emphasize the boundless nature of human creativity and the importance of embracing your own unique artistic expression and letting Your Angel be there to encourage you!

Creativity is a magical place, available to everyone, especially You!

What if... I fully embrace my own unique creativity and use it as a powerful tool for self-expression, healing, and navigating through this thing called life with the support of My Angel?

Dear Angel of Artistic Expressions, please release any self-doubt and guide me on my creative journey. Please inspire me to embrace the beauty of imperfection in all of my artistic expressions... or something better! Thank you for being my constant companion and source of guidance. Thank you, thank you, thank you.

Creative Practice

Doodle-ISH:

- Start by just drawing a DOT.

- Think of something you want to draw and from that dot, let go and begin to draw its ish-ness. If your drawing takes an unexpected turn, embrace it! Should the resemblance elude you, accompany it with words, as this provides instant context.

- **Unleash your Curiosità, release judgment, take the plunge, and witness the joy of doodle-ish.**

- Jump in! You got this!

Coming up next, what if… instead of trying to do things perfectly you were able to embrace the practice of progress…

Ask for help not because you're weak, but because you want to remain strong.

— *Les Brown*

Chapter 20

Lilly And The Angel

Creative Practice Part III

**What if instead of trying to write things perfectly,
I simply focus on expressing myself?**

Lilly & The Angel

In a land not too far away, there was a young girl named Lilly who had always believed in the presence of Angels. She had heard stories of their guidance and protection, and she longed to experience their support in her own life. One day, as she sat alone in her room, she decided to give voice to her desires.

Lilly took out a pen and paper and began writing a heartfelt letter to Her Angel. She poured out her hopes, dreams, and challenges, speaking out loud as she penned each word. With every stroke of the pen, she could feel a sense of connection growing stronger within her.

As days went by, Lilly continued her practice of speaking out loud to Her Angel. She shared her fears and doubts, her joys and aspirations. Sometimes she would go to a quiet place in nature, where she felt the presence of Her Angel most strongly. There, she would speak aloud, expressing her gratitude and asking for guidance.

Little did she know that her words were being heard. Her Angels listened attentively, their loving presence surrounding her with invisible wings. Through her spoken words, Lily opened a channel of communication between herself and Her Angel.

As time went on, Lilly began to notice subtle shifts in her life. She felt a greater sense of inner peace and clarity. Answers to her questions would often come to her in unexpected ways – through synchronicities, intuition, or signs in the world around her. She realized that by speaking out loud and writing to Her Angel, she was creating a space for Her Angel to always be with her.

Encouraged by her experiences, Lilly shared her newfound practice with others. She told them about the power of speaking out loud or writing out their desires, fears, and dreams. She encouraged them to connect with their own Angel, trusting that they too would receive the support and guidance they sought.

And so, the message spread like an autumn breeze, inspiring people to find their voice, to speak their truth, and to invite the loving presence of their Angel into their lives. Through the simple act of speaking out loud or writing it out, they discovered a profound connection and a renewed sense of faith in the Angels who walked WITH them.

And they lived knowing that their Angels were always there, patiently listening, ready to guide and uplift them as they journeyed through this adventure called life.

> ## Writing & Speaking Out Loud
>
> If you are wrapped up in a problem and want to shift your focus to the solution, here's how!
>
> - Write out what the problem is.
> - List out all of the possible solutions you can think of.
> - Then CROSS OUT all of the unrealistic solutions that expect others to change instead of you.
> - Ask for the solution, and if you don't know, you can always ask for what you think you want and then say, "OR SOMETHING BETTER."

Why "Or Something Better?" Sometimes we think we know exactly what we want, but what about those things that are outside of our thinking... what about opening up to something better than what you think you could ask for yourself?

If you are unable to write it down, then speak it all out loud, and always end with what you DO want.

EXAMPLE:

"Angel, I have this pain in my back and what I want is to feel healthy, happy, and mobile in my body again, or something better. Thank you, thank you, thank you!"

Do this while it is fresh in your mind, do the best you can. Think about exploring the "Asking" process and not waiting to be perfect with it.

> **Perfectionism will often get in the way of any progress. Let it be imperfect, just like life itself.**

"One of the basic rules of the universe is that NOTHING IS PERFECT. Perfection simply doesn't exist... without imperfection, neither you nor I would exist." — Stephen Hawking

This process is asking you to believe in Your Angel. It's asking you to believe that you deserve the things and relationships that you do want. It's asking you to believe that you deserve to feel good!

We are all here for a reason.

YES, we are ALL here for a reason. What Will You ASK of Your Angel?

Ask yourself, who do I fight with?

Do you fight with Yourself?

Do you fight with Others?

Can you hear both sides of the story?

Are you open to listening or have you shut down, convinced you are right and they are wrong?

> *"Yesterday I was so clever, so I wanted to change the world. Today I am wise, so I am changing myself."* — *Rumi*

When you speak out loud, it improves muscle memory and aids in remembering what it is you do want.

> **Speaking out loud helps to break the cycle of negative thoughts repeating over and over in your mind. Instead of letting your thoughts spin endlessly, speaking them out loud allows you to focus on them. It signals to your mind that you have processed those thoughts, rather than letting them loop-de-loop and hamster wheel in your mind throughout the day.**

I find that talking out loud and vocalizing my thoughts and emotions helps me move past those negative thoughts, therefore releasing the stress and anxiety that can often accompany negative thoughts. It serves as a valuable outlet for expressing myself even when there is no one else to listen or help me with an issue.

Writing is a powerful tool for getting clear on what you do want and what you don't want. It allows you to be specific and tap into your creative mind. Unlike thinking, which often repeats the same ideas over and over again, writing helps you move beyond negative repetition, get off the hamster wheel, and discover new ideas. **This process of reflecting on your thoughts through writing can help you quickly alleviate stress and anxiety.**

Through writing, you can reflect on your experiences, explore and express your emotions, and gain a deeper understanding of your values and beliefs. This self-awareness and self-knowledge can lead to feeling more confident and bring about a stronger sense of your own identity, values, and desires.

Writing enables you to reframe your thoughts, reinforce positive ideas, and ultimately remember the things you want to focus on.

Moreover, writing helps you stay focused on a task. It acknowledges that your mind tends to wander and jump from thought to thought like a monkey swinging from vine to vine to vine. So by p a u s i n g and consciously bringing your focus back to what you do want, writing can help you remove distractions so that you can focus more on what you do want.

Empowerment is in asking for help, and embracing the unseen support that surrounds you. Through writing and speaking out loud, you invite Your Angel into your life, opening doors to profound connections, inner peace, finding the answers, and t he realization that you are never alone.

This practice is asking you to believe in Your Angel. It's asking you to believe that you deserve the things and

relationships that you do want. It's asking you to believe that you deserve to feel good!

Asking Your Angel Practice

You can take the answer to these questions to create the following ASK of Your Angel!

→ **Dear Angel, I'm feeling** _____

Tell your angel exactly what you are feeling.

EXAMPLE: Angel, I'm feeling really angry and hopeless with the world right now, there is so much pain and suffering everywhere and I just can't carry it anymore, It hurts, I feel stuck and I just can't seem to get motivated because if feels like what's the point!

→ **I'd like to be feeling** _____

This is the turnaround, it's time to start focusing on the solution. Tell Your Angel what you would rather be feeling instead.

EXAMPLE: I want to feel good, like there is a reason to wake up and take in the sunshine. I want to feel happy and productive and finish my projects. I want to feel inspired and run around like a child without a care in the world except for the sensation of running around taking in the good things around me.

→ **Please take away (negative feeling/emotion/ pattern/habit)** _____

→ **List what you no longer want...**

EXAMPLE: I no longer want to feel angry at the world. I no longer want to feel sad about the world. I no longer want to feel like this life is just hopeless and I'm just not good enough.

→ **And replace it with _____**

BE specific and use powerful and descriptive words.

EXAMPLE: I want to feel happy, I want to feel free, I want to let go of all of the things that are out of my control, I want to feel like the world is a beautiful and amazing place, Or Something Better!

I like to end my requests with the statement "or something better."

Ending your ASK with OR SOMETHING BETTER helps you break out of your own limitations. I touched on this a little bit back in Chapter 15, "The Wise Farmer."

Why should you limit yourself to what you think is the best thing out there? **What if there is something so much better or more useful that you haven't even thought of yet?**

Asking for this or something better sets you up for the best of the best. Then have faith that Your Angel will provide and will most likely provide something even better than what you thought to ASK for.

Perhaps Your Angel has something better in store for you than you even have the confidence to ask for… ask for what you want and then be open to that or something even better…

EXAMPLE: I want to feel happy and energetic or something better!

→ **What I'm willing to do for this is** _____

This can be as simple as I'm willing to turn to you for guidance, I'm willing to write about it, I'm willing to get out of this situation and get into nature, I'm willing to sit here and feel your presence, I'm willing to watch a funny movie to get into a different state of mind, etc.. etc.. etc…

EXAMPLE: I'm willing to write to you, to give all of these fears and worries to you in this writing and then I'm willing to close this book for now and walk away and start working on one little thing that I'm passionate about (such as painting, gardening, nature or any of the creative practices).

As mentioned previously, I like to end my asks with a Thank You! Just as you would for someone taking on the burden of carrying a heavy backpack for you - that heaviness within - you can hand it over to Your Angel…they will carry it for you, and when you say thank you, you acknowledge that they are helping, that you are being helped, and that you are not alone. **(This is powerful)**

EXAMPLE: Thank you, Thank you, Thank you for listening to me, I already feel better getting this out and asking for better feelings.

For simplicity, Here is the process again:

→ Dear Angel, I'm feeling _____

→ I'd like to be feeling _____

→ Please take away (negative feeling/emotion/pattern/habit) _____

→ List what you no longer want _____

→ And replace it with _____

→ What I'm willing to do for this is _____

There are so many people and their contributions have played a transformative role in shaping my life, and ultimately have helped me bring this book together. Among these incredible teachers, is Byron Katie, renowned for her teachings on self-inquiry as outlined in her brilliant book, "The Work."

Byron Katie's profound insights and methodologies for self-inquiry have been instrumental in my life. She offers a framework that encourages deep introspection, offering powerful tools to understand and challenge one's thought patterns. Her insights remind me of that old victim mindset and how to break free from it. I believe that her work has been ingrained in me leading to the creation of this format for Asking Your Angel. So Thank You, Thank You, Thank You Angel Byron Katie for this inspiration and all of the gifts and liberation you bring to this world!

"To find your angels… Start trusting your inner voice and intuition." — Melanie Beckler

What Do You Wish For?

ASK Your Angel with childlike abandonment. They are there for you, loving you, adoring you, and whispering to you, "Your wish is my command."

> **If your thoughts are all full of fears, that is what Your Angel thinks you are wishing for. Read that again!**

 "You get what you focus on. So focus on what you want." — Steve Mehr

Angels are Messengers and Reflectors. Sometimes they try to intervene to help you move past your limitations. But, you must be willing to meet them in that space for them to truly help you. You can start by asking for what you DO want, focusing on what you DO want… and begin to LET GO of the story of what you don't want.

What Will You Ask Of Your Angel?

Go ahead and ASK!

With time and practice, you will believe more and more as you see the results from asking Your Angel for help.

Give it time, give it attention, be persistent with it, and put your heart into it.

> *"We all have at least two sides. The world we live in is a world of opposites. And the trick is to reconcile those opposing things. I've always liked both sides. In order to appreciate one you have to know the other. The more darkness you can gather up, the more light you can see too."*
> — *David Lynch*

In the dance of opposites, through writing and speaking out loud, you unlock the door to a more harmonious way of living, inviting Your Angel to guide you through the depths of darkness and to illuminate your path, finding the lightness and joy along your journey.

The Power & Harmony Of Writing

> *"Writing is like breathing, it's possible to learn to do it well, but the point is to do it no matter what."* — *Julia Cameron*

The story of Judy Blume and her near encounter with throwing her typewriter away is an anecdote that reflects the challenges and frustrations faced by the beloved author during her writing journey.

As Judy explains " I got a nasty review once for a book I wrote and it really got to me. In a moment of sheer frustration, I contemplated tossing my typewriter into the arroyo." As if to symbolically rid herself of the perceived failure. It was a moment of despair and doubt, where the weight of her creative struggles felt unbearable.

Then a little voice (perhaps an Angel) said to her "Wait, you are going to let this one review stop you from writing? That's crazy, that's one opinion!"

Thankfully, Judy did not give in to that impulse and instead listened to that little Angel in her head which gave her the determination to continue writing.

This anecdote serves as a reminder of the ups and downs faced by many writers and creative individuals. It highlights the frustrations and doubts that can arise during the creative practice, but also the resilience and tenacity required to overcome them. Judy Blume's story inspires aspiring writers to push through obstacles, embrace their passion, and keep pursuing their dreams, even when the journey feels daunting. Continue to preserve the gems through the rubble.

Writing

"We should write because it is human nature to write. Writing claims our world. It makes it directly and specifically our own. We should write because humans are spiritual beings and writing is a powerful form of prayer and meditation, connecting us both to our own insights and to a higher and deeper level of inner guidance.

We should write because writing brings clarity and passion to the act of living. Writing is sensual, experiential, grounding. We should write because writing is good for the soul. We should write because writing yields us a body of work, a felt path through the world we live in.

> *We should write, above all, because we are writers, whether we call ourselves that or not."*
> — Julia Cameron – The Right to Write

Writing is creativity, it taps into a different part of your brain than thinking or speaking.

Creative writing is letting your connection to your intuition and Your Angel pour through you with a pen (or pencil) and paper.

• ♥ • ♥ • ♥ • ♥ • ♥ •

Angel Writing

Have you ever heard of automatic writing? As a kid, I found a companion in writing because I didn't know who else to turn to or what else to do with all of my emotions.

Despite my troubled thoughts, putting pen to paper brought me comfort. At the time, I didn't realize there was a technical term for what I was doing, but now I understand that much of my writing would fall under the category of "automatic writing."

Automatic writing is a process that taps into your subconscious mind, allowing thoughts, ideas, and words to effortlessly flow onto paper without conscious control. It's a form of writing where you enter a relaxed state and let your hand move freely, seemingly guided by Your Angel into your own subconscious mind. I now refer to it as Angel Writing.

If You Want To Experience Angel Writing (or Automatic Writing), Give This A Try

- Find a quiet and comfortable place where you can write without distractions. Have pen and paper ready.

- Take a few deep breaths to allow your mind and body to relax and become present.

- Set an intention for your writing session. You can set the intention that you are looking for guidance to resolve a problem, that you want more access to your creative mind, to explore and let go of emotions or anything else you have in mind.

- Allow yourself to let go and just start writing without consciously controlling or judging the words that appear on the paper. Allow your hand to move freely, letting thoughts, ideas, and words flow naturally. Don't worry about grammar, spelling, or punctuation; the focus is on allowing the stream of consciousness to guide your writing.

- Maintain a state of detachment from the words that emerge on the page. Avoid analyzing or criticizing what you are writing. Remind yourself to let go and keep the pen moving. **It's Super Important to ignore grammar, spelling, and punctuation.** Let the focus be on the stream of consciousness as your pen keeps moving on the paper.

- Write until you reach a natural stopping point. At first, you may just write a few sentences and feel done, but eventually, when you engage in this more and more you will find that so much more wants to flow onto your paper.

- Be patient if you're new to Angel Writing. It may take a few attempts to get into the flow and fully experience the practice. Sometimes, you may already be doing it without realizing it, just like driving home on autopilot.

- After completing your writing session, write down a few words that express your feelings. I often feel relieved and ready to move on with my day after an Angel Writing session. I like to end each writing with a heartfelt "Thank you, thank you, thank you." I express gratitude for My Angel helping me with this process, and for the emotions and feelings that have been released.

As for what to do with these writings… In my 30s, I found myself overwhelmed with seven banker boxes filled to the brim with writings I had accumulated since I was around 13 years old. Initially, I believed these writings held significant meaning, but upon reflection and before discovering the methods explained in this book, I realized that much of what I wrote was negative, whiny, and full of complaints. It was truly a time for ch-ch-change.

As discussed in Chapter 11, "It's A Wonderful Life", where I emphasized the importance of breaking free from the victim mindset, I understood that I needed to release the burden of carrying around this baggage of complaints from place to place. Motivated to let go, not long after my encounter with the concept of "stop being a victim," I set sail on a mission.

I lived in the Pacific Northwest at the time and chose a serene campsite as the backdrop for my transformative act. Over the course of an entire day, I intentionally tore out the pages from each notebook, from each box, one by one, and set them ablaze. The flames and pile of ashes eventually consumed all seven banker boxes of writings, symbolizing the release of the negative energy they held over me. As the last of the pages crumbled in red and black ashes, I immersed my hands in the nearby river, metaphorically cleansing myself of the heavy baggage and accumulated inner dust I had lugged for so long.

I recognized that the essence of this accumulated negativity could only be fully released by letting go of the writings themselves. Although I occasionally wrote poetry and perhaps there were a few gems in there that would remind me of special times, it was a gratifying decision to liberate myself from years of anxiety, depression, feeling like a victim, and constant complaining. Tougher was later that year when I also thought it beneficial to rid myself of most of my previous artworks as well.

Now, when I write, I swiftly release any negativity and redirect my focus toward what I truly desire.

Looking back on these writings, I gained invaluable insight into my personal growth and the progress (not perfection) I have made. By asking for what I want and relinquishing what no longer serves me, I have transformed my relationship with writing into a tool for positive change and self-expression.

You are free to do what you want with writings and Angel Writings. If I'm looking for change or transformation, I usually keep them as a reminder. When it's just to release anger or negativity, I often write them on a loose piece of paper and then tear it up into little shreds and throw them away… or if there is going to be a campfire somewhere, I can accumulate the torn pieces of paper and then release them into the fire.

In the words of Julia Cameron, "Writing is like breathing, it's possible to learn to do it well, but the point is to do it no matter what." This quote emphasizes the importance of embracing the writing practice and expressing yourself authentically. Just as Judy Blume persevered through the challenges of her writing journey, I want to encourage you to push through obstacles, tap into your creativity, and let go of perfectionism. By embracing imperfection and allowing ideas to flow freely, the Creative Practices will become a powerful tool for self-discovery and personal growth. Use the Angel Writing practice to help you embrace this more and more and more.

"People try so hard to let go of their negative behaviors and thoughts, and it doesn't work, or it works only for a short time. I didn't let go of my negative thoughts, I questioned them, and then they let go of me, and so did my addictions and depression." — Byron Katie

In this chapter, we explored the importance of writing and speaking out loud to amplify your intentions and desires. The story of Lilly, a young girl who believed in Angels, serves as inspiration for connecting with Your Angel through writing and speaking out loud. By writing out problems, listing possible solutions, and asking for guidance, you can open a channel of communication with Your Angel. These practices encourage strengthening your belief and communication with Your Angel, knowing your self-worth, and opening up to the possibility of receiving something even better than what you asked for. By embracing both sides of life and using the power of writing and speaking, you can bridge opposing forces and find harmony within yourself.

What if... I embraced all sides of life
and used the power of writing and
speaking out loud to find
creative solutions?

Dear Angel of Writing,
let me pour out my hopes,
dreams, and challenges,
writing to you from my
heart. I trust that you will
guide me along my path
while also protecting me... or something even better!
Thank you, thank you, thank you.

Creative Practice

Angel Writing Exploration:

- Grab a pen and paper; set a timer for just 5 minutes. Begin to let go and write!

- Angel Writing is the act of writing continuously without worrying about grammar, spelling, or punctuation.

- Let your thoughts cascade freely on the page, exploring various ideas, scenarios, or perspectives tied to the possibilities you wish to uncover in your mind.

- This exercise opens the door to your creative flow, offering you a pathway to the unexplored mental landscapes in your subconscious mind. Embrace the spontaneity and see where your thoughts lead you during this insightful journey. Let go and jump in!

In the next chapter, let's find out how Your Angel can help you with any creative practice you desire…

It's not about finding your voice, it's about giving yourself permission to use your voice.

— *Kris Carr*

Chapter 21

The Angel Doll

Creative Practice Part IV

How can My Angel help me with My Creative Practice?

The Angel Doll

In 2020 during that difficult time, I was part of a collaborative paper doll project and it became clear, that my contribution would be a Paper Angel Doll. There were many reasons, the biggest one being that I really needed to know that My Angel was with me, and the best way I knew to do that was to have her in visual form. This process was so healing, that for many weeks, I was able to lose myself in the creative practice, therefore bringing her to reality.

Once she was complete, I thought - She is here to listen, to love you, and to help you through anything and everything you want or need help with.

I hung the various versions of her up on the wall, and I must say it was quite difficult to ship them off. But they were meant to be shared, so I sent them off with love and care.

The response I got from these Angels touched me so much, and it was my dear ol' Dad who first recommended that it be turned into a book!

That creative practice led to making a holiday card for the next year and now into this book!

> *"As you embrace your deepest nature, the energies of your being shine forth into your body, your mind, and your world."* — Donna Eden

As I look at this Angel Doll, I see so much that I want to redo! Yet how would I know this if I had not yet arrived at this point?

So here she is, in her perfect imperfections– like life, like Mother Earth, like Father Sky, like me, like you.

She knows that we are just oh so human. The Angels, at times, laugh with us, like a patient teacher or parent might towards a child for doing something that seems silly in the adult mind. She watches as that child navigates its growth, obstacles, and exploration through the world.

Her Face: I struggled to draw her face. She has her "Am I enough?" issues. She asks "Am I pretty enough or creative enough? Do I exude what an Angel should be… enough? Do I carry the messages enough? Will I get through and bring good? Am I even good enough to bring good? Am I good enough to be considered an Angel?"

Does the "Am I enoughness" sound familiar? Am I good enough, pretty enough, smart enough, loveable enough?

As with any practice, it is one of learning and growing. I could start this Angel painting over again and again, but there is something that she communicates. So I had to stop and listen. Do you know how to listen? As perfectly, imperfect as she is… just like us.

Angel Body: The button through her heart bouquet represents all that we hold together and mend. All of our hurts and wants. All of the feelings we try to keep bottled up because we are afraid of what might be revealed. All of the dreams not yet manifested, maybe even the dreams we've let go of because of time, because of beliefs that it's too late? Because I'm not enough? Sometimes life feels just day-to-day and that we are dangling on a thin string. Other days we are strong, solid, and stitched in tight.

Skirt: Her skirt, all the colors of humanity. Oh, how beautiful when we can come together. It's the blending of peace. It's being able to look at all sides and wonder more about how others came to their beliefs. Why do they believe differently? And what led up to that? What can I learn from them? It doesn't mean you believe what others do…but more so you gather information from all sides so that you can create a belief that feels harmonious and balanced to you.

Can we move past our differences and come together?
Can we work together, and stop tearing one another down?
Can we learn to lift each other up?

"The thing is, we have to let go of all blame, all attacking, all judging, to free our inner selves to attract what we say we want. Until we do, we are hamsters in a cage chasing our own tails and wondering why we aren't getting the results we seek." — Dr. Joe Vitale

Wings: The wings represent what we all have within us; a childlike belief and a knowing that anything is possible. A child BELIEVES with all its being in the power of wings in motion. It may watch a bug intently or feel its "imaginary friend" nearby… a child will believe until that belief is broken. Let's go back, mend these wings, and believe again like we did as a child before that spell was broken for us or out of us?

When a child BELIEVES, you can see it in their face when they light up talking about it… why do so many experience these wings being ripped off of them?

Metal Heart: The heart that she holds is the "bouquet" that we gather throughout our lives. Often, we hold onto experiences such as traumas, journeys, joys, loves, and griefs that mold us into who and what we think we are today. We must own who we are without hiding, being proud of our lines, our scars, our aging, and our personal journey.

The metal heart is the one we wear out loud. It creates the lines on our faces and the words from our hearts. The Angels can help us share our hearts out loud like well-cared-for flowers.

May we all be able to share our hearts out loud and offer them like beautiful flowers that we know will be well cared for. **Knowing that seeds are plentiful and that we will replenish after each and every hurt. We have that power.** Your Angel can help.

What Is This Angel Doll's Definition of Love?:
Love is unconditional. It begins with loving yourself unconditionally. How do you love yourself unconditionally? Remember, this whole book is about how you can Ask Your Angel to help you love yourself unconditionally.

Love might be different than we've been led to believe.
Love is letting go. Love is giving. Love is kindness.
Love is receiving.

Love is not expecting others to change. Rather it is for you to love yourself enough to accept others as they are; to accept yourself as you are. It is self-love that allows you to stay with or move away from others.

What Is This Angel Doll's Definition Of Hope?:
There are different definitions. For me "Hope" is the childlike innocence of believing that the world or a situation will be okay.

Hope is that essence of The Angel… knowing that within us is pure love, pure magic. I'd call it faith in The Angels.

"Creative success means balancing your love of starting things with a habit of finishing them."
— *Marie Forleo*

This chapter is dedicated to the Creative Practice of The Angel Doll, and really any Creative Practice. This Angel Doll helped me through some really difficult times and was a way to heal and connect with the presence and gifts of My Angel. I shared with you the different elements of the Angel Doll as they came about while creating her, including her imperfect yet meaningful appearance, the representation of healing and emotions, unity and understanding, childlike belief, and the experiences that shape us. This practice also explored the Angel Doll's perspective on love as unconditional and hope as the childlike belief in a positive outcome. I now invite YOU to engage in any of the Creative Practices, inviting in the assistance of Your Angel for Creative Expression and Freedom!

What if... I turned to any of the creative practices and gave myself permission to express myself authentically?

Dear Angel of Imagination, please give me the freedom and inspiration to create no matter how big or how small... or something better! Thank you, thank you, thank you.

Creative Practice

Angel Art Doodle:

- 💛 Draw or doodle on or around the provided Heart with wings illustration.

- 💛 Or, draw or find a picture of your own rendition of An Angel.

- 💛 Let your artistic expression bring life to Your Angel. Allow the process to be a reflection of your own perception and connection with Your Angel.

Moving right along, what if… you could have creative inspiration every day…

Energy can't be created or destroyed, and energy flows. It must be in a direction, with some kind of internal, emotive, spiritual direction. It must have some effect somewhere.

— *Keanu Reeves*

Chapter 22
Creativity Like A Dance

Creative Practice Part V

How is Creativity Like Energy?

Creativity – Like A Dance

Creativity is a space and place that calls for a certain action. That action is not always intentional, but the space asks for it. The space is trained to encourage certain involvement. We instinctively know when we enter a library to shussshh; we know when we've stepped into a sacred creative space to stop and take it in, and to feeeeeeeeel it. Often we can notice it taking over us and moving us through it, almost involuntarily... like a dance.

I've lived in small studio apartments, where everything had multiple functions. When in small spaces I dreamed beyond those cramped quarters towards a large spacious studio, but no matter how limited in space, still I created.

Even when every content of my life had to fit into my car, there was always a sketchbook handy. All these spaces urge us to create. There is no waiting for the perfect place to create. You must create for that perfect space to be energetically called in. You are in its forward motion, calling out for it by doing the creative dance now!

I've waited for a space like this for most of my life. Sometimes, it's hard to believe that it's truly mine to do with as I please. The practice of creating an Inspiration Wall is vital and it sets down a sense of roots that didn't exist just years ago when pieces were stored away in boxes and cabinets, out of sight.

I began to create this space and then, like being on the dance floor with my favorite song, the music takes over my body and I'm just moving. It's the same as being in 'the zone' — the creative actions took over the space and began to create itself.

It started with just one picture, which inspired another, sent me to another pile to choose from, and just like that… just like an idea forms on the sketchbook and then into a painting, the wall presented itself. This wall now welcomes me into my true space. A place where I can open and close the door as I choose. I can draw, paint, sculpt, and create in this place as I desire.

I know that creativity goes with me like a purse wherever I go… and yet, there is something enchanting about unpacking, having a place for everything, and being inspired from the moment I walk in that still feels magical. This kind of thing is something that I've only observed in other people's studios, not in myself or in my own space… that is until now. Now, when I enter into this room — my room, my creative and working space — it feels more and more like the place where I truly belong.

The more willing I am to unpack these things from within me for others to see and invest my time in, the more this space becomes an authentic reflection of who I want to be… an artist!

This room, this creative space, this mysterious wall of decades of my own work and works that inspire me… lives and breathes on its own.

As I enter, it welcomes me with **Curiosità**, wonder, and the forward movement of the practices I've put into place all these years. It asks me 'What next shall we collaborate on?' It feels as if I've stepped into the most majestic dance hall, surrounded by loving friends and family, with music pulsing through my body, moving me to the beat regardless of my mood.

And just like these wonderful friends and family, I sense their presence here. They welcome me with boundless supplies and ideas, beckoning me to join them on the dance floor of creativity!

This writing, Creativity—Like A Dance… was inspired by the Inspiration Wall I created for my office. I was inspired by Mixed Media Artist Seth Apter, and this process ultimately led me to be part of his Fall 2022 article in the Magazine "Where Women Create."

"When we consciously step onto the platform of creativity, innovative magic happens within our lives over and over." — Debbie Rosas

Creating An Inspiration Wall

An Inspirational Wall is a physical space in your home, office, or studio where you display pictures, drawings, images, quotes, trinkets, and any other visuals that inspire you. I call it an Inspiration Wall, but that doesn't mean you have to fill the entire wall, it can be very small or very large, depending on what you have the space, time, and energy for. The Inspiration Wall gives you a visual reminder of your creativity, your goals, dreams, and keeps you motivated and focused on them because they take up space in your home/studio/workspace.

To create your own Inspiration Wall, begin by choosing a location for it. It could be a small space such as a corkboard or a large space such as a wall, a bulletin board, a whiteboard, etc.

Next, gather inspiration from various sources. It can be your own writings and works of art or pieces you print from the internet, find in magazines, books, photos, etc. Choose the items that give you a sense of inspiration and that you love looking at. These things should align with your passions, goals, and values.

Arrange your inspirational pieces on the board. You can tack them up to make sure that's where you want them or just go for it and tape them down, pin them down, or whatever works for the substrate you are using.

There are many board-like-things you can use:

- ♥ Corkboard is great as you can use push pins to hold your items in place.

- ♥ Magnetic Boards with strong magnets are wonderful if you don't want to put holes or tape onto your items.

- ♥ Whiteboards are great to use with tape, this works well when creating a collage effect because you don't see the push pins or magnets.

Arrange your inspirational items on your chosen surface and begin to move items around to see what works best for you.

There are many approaches to your inspiration board, and how you approach it depends on your own personality, the time you want to put into it, and what you want it to INSPIRE in you!

Some people choose to update their Inspirational Wall each year, some people pop it up, and it remains like a piece of artwork on the wall. Allow the Inspirational Wall to speak to you and create it, leave it, or change it whenever you are inspired to do so.

The key is to have items on your Inspirational Wall that speak to you, moves you toward the feelings you DO want, and brings the creative spark you want as well as the daily inspiration that will move you toward your creative desires and goals.

Your Inspiration Wall is a powerful collaged work of art that can help you stay focused and motivated. It can also set the tone of your space.

Put some thought into how you want this wall to feel. I have often created very "dark art" as a way of expression, and while I love these pieces, I also don't want to feel depressed or experience that dark feeling every time I walk into the room, so I truly balance them with things that are uplifting, colorful and inspiring.

> *"Thoughts are an important part of your inner wisdom and they are very powerful. A thought held long enough and repeated often enough becomes a belief. A belief then becomes your biology."* — Dr. Christiane Northup

In this quote by Dr. Northup, shares profound wisdom that thoughts become beliefs, and if you want something to become a belief, you must have thoughts about it, and what better way than to surround yourself with images that produce those very thoughts that you want!

This chapter hopes to inspire you to create your own inspiration space, as it's a fantastic way to boost creativity and motivation. No matter how large or tiny a space you have, you can do

CREATIVITY LIKE A DANCE

this! Fill it with artworks, images, and quotes that inspire you and serve as a constant reminder of your goals and dreams. Remember that thoughts become beliefs, so surround yourself with visuals that evoke positive emotions. Give it a try and see how it shifts the energy from what you don't want into what you DO want!

Nicole White
is a self-proclaimed wild, Wild West mixed-media artist in New Mexico. For Nicole, the process of creating an inspiration board "sets down a sense of roots that was not there just months ago, as pieces were stuffed away in boxes and cabinets, out of view. It started with just one picture, which inspired another, and just like that ... just like an idea forms on the sketchbook and then into a painting, the wall presented itself." Creating this board has now changed how Nicole feels about her space. "This room, this creative space, this amazing wall of decades of my own work and works that inspire me, lives and breathes on its own."

www.RavenArtCenter.com | **Email:** ravenartcenter@gmail.com

What if... I found a place within my space to create an Inspiration Board or Wall?

Dear Angel of Inspiration, let me bring in this Inspirational Wall (or whatever space you have) and fill it with visuals that create the emotions I WANT to feel in this space. Please help this space inspire me, keep me motivated and wildly creative... or something better! Thank you, thank you, thank you.

Creative Practice

Angel Art Doodle:

- Doodle or write out some things that ignite inspiration for you. Let this be the beginning or continuation of your journey to cultivate inspiration in your own personal space!

- Plan and envision, or dive right in to create your very own Inspirational Wall or Creativity-Inspired piece!

- Let your creative spirit guide the practice, turning your inspirations into tangible expressions.

Continuing onward, So… you are looking for ways to heal what ails you eh?… Yes, let's walk through those possibilities in the next chapter…

Your authentic, true self doesn't lie to you, mislead you, or take you away from your power source.

— *Dr. Christiane Northup*

Chapter 23

Dear Art Angel

Creative Practice Part VI

How do I tap into creativity for health, fulfillment, and healing?

Art Journaling Is An Anything-Goes Process

Art journaling is a versatile and Creative Practice that can be adapted to suit your personality and needs. Whether you're an experienced artist or a beginner, it offers a welcoming space for creative exploration and personal expression.

I have been Art Journaling for decades. Mine is very simple: A sketchbook and a pen or pencil. I put my ideas in there, I draw, doodle, and write in them. I make dots and ish-drawings. I have a small one that I can fit into my purse and carry around with me, I have one by my bedside and one in my office. They are always there for me, and I turn to them just about every day, and sometimes multiple times a day. This is not finished artwork; these are IDEAS and allowing myself to play and to just let go and be myself.

My Art Journal gives me a space to put down all of my ideas, and I have an endless supply of original sketches to create artworks from because of those journals. My Art Journal is how I came up with the Angel Doll, which then became a story, which then evolved into this book and into the next section of Angel Art Journaling.

> **If I were to encourage just one Creative Practice, it would be to begin Art Journaling in any way that works for you. Let yourself get a notebook or blank-page sketchbook. Keep it with you, let it follow you around like a puppy. Let it become a habit, and you'll be amazed at what becomes of it and how it starts to serve you and your creativity!**

Art Journaling is a naturally creative and expressive practice that involves using a paper journal or notebook as a canvas for combining written words, drawings, paintings, collage, and various art materials to document thoughts, emotions, experiences, and ideas. It's a highly individualized form of self-expression and self-discovery, and it offers numerous benefits. Here's a brief description of Art Journaling.

CHOOSING YOUR MATERIALS: Gather any art supplies that call to you. I tend to keep it simple such as pens, pencils, colored pencils, and/or markers. Yours can be any materials you love!

- **Creating Pages:** Begin with a blank page or spread in your journal. You can either start with an idea you have, or begin with writing a word, or just draw a dot or a line and let your creativity flow spontaneously.

- **Combining Visuals & Words:** Express your thoughts, feelings, or experiences on the page through a combination of written words, doodles, ish-drawings, paintings, or collages. You can write journal entries, poetry, collect quotes, or simply doodle and experiment with colors.

- **Exploring Themes:** Your art journal can explore various themes, such as emotions, dreams, memories, daily life, travel experiences, or any subject that resonates with you.

- **Experimentation & Play:** Art journaling encourages experimentation and play. You can try new techniques, styles, and materials without the pressure of creating a finished piece of artwork.

- **Reflecting & Processing:** Use your art journal as a tool for self-reflection and processing. It allows you to visually represent your inner thoughts and emotions, making it easier to understand and work through them.

Art Journaling is a transformative Creative Practice. It provides a nurturing and expressive space for you to doodle, write, and capture memories. It's truly limitless what you can do with Art Journaling. Art Journaling serves as a stress-relieving, relaxation-promoting activity, anchoring you in the present moment. It acts as a powerful tool for releasing stored emotions, offering clarity on complex feelings, and facilitating your healing journey.

Art Journaling acts as a catalyst for enhancing creativity, encouraging experimentation, and helping you be more expansive in your thinking. It's a journey of self-discovery, unveiling hidden talents, uncovering patterns in thoughts and feelings, and providing insight into your own personal development and enrichment. Art Journaling offers you a positive and constructive way to channel energy and emotions, cultivating a sense of accomplishment and satisfaction. Through the creation and reflection upon your Art Journal pages, you can increase self-awareness, gain deeper insights into your desires and goals, and ultimately pave the way for a much happier and more fulfilling life! Art Journaling can really be that powerful!

Angel Art Journaling

Angel Art Journaling is my favorite go-to Art Journaling practice whenever I need quick relief from something that is going all cattywampus. It's also a great practice to use for anything that you want to create, accomplish, or let go of. Angel Art Journaling is the quickest way I know (along with breathing and shaking) to relieve stress and anxiety by getting it out onto the page and asking for relief.

Angel Art Journaling is a deeply intuitive, creative, and therapeutic process that allows you to connect with Your Angels, seek guidance, and express your thoughts, emotions, and desires through writing and drawing. It's a unique form of self-discovery and communication that builds a profound sense of connection and healing.

How It Works:

- **Art Journal or Paper:** Start with a blank page or space in your Art Journal or Journal. You can use any type of paper, loose paper, journal, or sketchbook that works for you, lined or blank.

- **Drawing Your Angel:** Begin by drawing or doodling something that feels like a symbol of Your Angel on the page. Your Angel can be as simple or intricate as you like. Draw an Angel-ISH (Chapter 19, "ISH") The intention is all that matters. I will often just start with a heart, simple and to the point.

- **Writing To Your Angel:** Below or around the image of Your Angel, write a letter or message to Your Angel. Share your thoughts, feelings, fears, desires, or requests. Be honest and open in your communication, as if you were having a conversation with a dear friend.

- **Expressing Emotions:** Use colors, shapes, or symbols in your artwork to represent your emotions and intentions. You can paint, color, use colored pencils, or incorporate collage elements that resonate with your message.

- **Gratitude & Release:** Express gratitude to Your Angel for their guidance and support. Release any worries or burdens onto the page, trusting that Your Angel will help you carry them.

- **Closing:** Close your Angel Art Journaling session with a sense of gratitude and peace. Thank Your Angel for their presence and assistance.

EXAMPLE: Here is a sample page of how I often Art Angel Journal: This process is also detailed in previous chapters.

- Dear Angel of Worry,
- I'm feeling overwhelmed with worry.
- I'd like to be feeling free, confident, and like I can breathe deeply again!
- Please help take away this feeling of anxiety and overwhelm and help me focus on feeling happy and free again
- Or something better
- Thank you, thank you, thank you!

To me, this one is simple, quick, and effective, and it's my go-to when any kind of difficult or unwanted issue happens in my life.

I encourage you to start with a blank page, draw a simple Angel-ISH drawing, and more importantly write to Your Angel.

The benefits of Angel Art Journaling are endless. It can help you stay and feel more connected to Your Angel. It provides an outlet for seeking guidance, healing, and comfort from Your Angel. It helps you release emotions, fears, and worries, providing more emotional clarity. This practice empowers you to take an active role in your emotional well-being, fostering a sense of empowerment and self-enrichment. Angel Art Journaling helps you explore drawing and doodling more by using symbols and ISH drawings. It gives you positive energy letting you be more empowered to ask for what you need and want.

Angel Art Journaling is a personal and sacred practice that can be deeply transformative. It provides a meaningful way to seek guidance, express your emotions, and nurture your connection with Your Angel.

Overall, Art Journaling or Angel Art Journaling can be a valuable tool for self-care and personal expansion. It will provide a creative outlet for stress relief, increase self-awareness, improve creativity, enhance problem-solving skills, and promote an overall sense of well-being and expansion.

 "We cannot cure the world of sorrows, but we can choose to live in joy." — Joseph Campbell

This chapter introduces Art Journaling and Angel Art Journaling as a liberating way to express yourself and seek guidance from Your Angel. Art Journaling involves words, drawings, pictures, or anything you can imagine, offering freedom and self-expression.

The practice of Angel Art Journaling enables you to quickly connect with Your Angel as you seek help and share your feelings.

There are numerous benefits to Art Journaling and Angel Art Journaling, such as reducing stress, increasing self-awareness, enhancing creativity, improving problem-solving skills, and so much more.

By incorporating these practices, you can use Art Journaling or Angel Art Journaling to gain insights into your thoughts and feelings and is a quick and easy way to connect with Your Angel. Allow these practices to bring you joy and even more creativity!

This chapter concludes by emphasizing the importance of giving yourself permission to express your creativity and embrace the guidance and magical friendship of Your Angel to cultivate creativity, follow your passions, and experience more joy, freedom, and transformation!

Now that we've explored
various Creative Practices,
what do you choose?

An Inspiration Wall,
Art Journaling,
Angel Art Journaling,
Writing, Cooking,
Gardening, Dancing,
Music, or something else???

Find a Creative Practice that
resonates with you and explore it
as much as possible!

What if... I let myself create an Art Journal? What if I was free to write, draw, doodle, collect, and/or collage in it in any way? What if this was just for me and I let myself be a kid again, creating wildly and freely?

Dear Angel of Art Journaling, please let me turn to Art Journaling and Angel Art Journaling more and more and more! Let me pour out my heart and my emotions into it, and seek guidance and solutions through it... or something better! Thank you, thank you, thank you!

Creative Practice

Art Journal Visioning:

- Grab a journal or a piece of paper. Write down or doodle about what you would like an Art journal to look like for you.

- Start simple, exploring the various possibilities and creative avenues you can take.

- Initiate the practice in a way that feels calm, comforting, and expressive for you.

- Let the vision of your Art Journal unfold on the pages, guided by Your Angel and your inner creative intuition.

In the next pages, let's find out what to do if you are not feeling well or are sick…

Inside any deep asking is the answering.

— *Rumi*

Chapter 24

When You Wish Upon A Star

Seeking Help From Your Angel When Feeling Unwell

How can My Angel help me when I'm not feeling well or facing illness?

When You Wish Upon A Star

The song "When You Wish Upon a Star" was written by Leigh Harline and Ned Washington. It was composed for the Walt Disney animated film "Pinocchio" released in 1940.

"When you wish upon a star
Makes no difference who you are
Anything your heart desires

267

Will come to you
If your heart is in your dream
No request is too extreme
When you wish upon a star
As dreamers do
Fate is kind
She brings to those who love
The sweet fulfillment of their secret longing
Like a bolt out of the blue
Fate steps in and sees you through
When you wish upon a star
Your dreams come true"

I've always loved this song, it brings in a sense of wonder and joy, and the remembering of looking up into the starry sky. The whole point of the song is to make a wish, which is asking for something that you want. The secret to this song is to dream, wish, ask and then you also need to take inspired action for what you wish for.

Transformational Asking!

We started the Asking Journey from the beginning, and in Chapter 11 with Angel Clarence, which dives into the details of Mastering The Art Of Asking as well as the Ask & Action Method. Here we continue your Asking Journey because it's ESSENTIAL in helping you get what you want. Becoming an Alchemist is defined as a person who transforms or creates something through a seemingly magical process.

That's what Asking Your Angel is... it's MAGICAL and it's TRANSFORMATIONAL!

Ask for what you wish for and then share with Your Angel what you want and what will do for it.

ASK Your Angel with childlike abandonment. She is there for you, loving you, adoring you, and whispering to you, **"Your wish is my command."**

If your thoughts are all full of fears, that is what Your Angel thinks you are wishing for. ← Read that again!

Angels are Messengers and Reflectors. Sometimes they try to intervene to help you move past your limitations. But, you must be willing to meet them in that space for them to truly help you. You can start by asking for what you DO want, focusing on what you DO want... and begin to LET GO of the story of what you don't want.

What will you ask of Your Angel?

As Jack Canfield and Mark Victor Hansen would say "Ask, Ask, Ask!"

 "You have nothing to lose and everything to gain by asking." — *Jack Canfield*

In time and with practice, you will believe more and more as you see results from asking Your Angel for help.

Give it time, give it attention, be persistent with it, and put your heart into it.

"Plant your seeds. Water them. Do your part as best as you can. The Universe will do it's part perfectly every time, no exceptions."
— John Assaraf

> **Remember that when asking for what YOU want, you are not asking for someone else to change! YOU are asking for what YOU need to do or possess in order for the situation or problem to change, be resolved, or be released!**

Can you ask to change yourself, your attitude, or your attention towards the problem? **YES!**

Can you ask to be relieved of an emotion? **YES!**

Can you ask to feel better, receive clarity, or shift your focus away from the problem? **YES!**

I used to ask for others to change until I learned that trying to change and, therefore, control others was a waste of time and energy, and frankly didn't work!

"The only time you can change someone is when they are in diapers." —Mark Victor Hansen.

Which Do You Choose?

> **Remember, Angels are Messengers, here to help you, and all you have to do is ASK!**

Start right now; not tomorrow. Your future begins today, not tomorrow. Take that first step towards your dreams now and let your journey begin to surprise you in a delightful way.

> *"Whenever we feel lost, or insane, or afraid, all we have to do is ask for His help. The help might not come in the form we expected, or even thought we desired, but it will come, and we will recognize it by how we feel inside. In spite of everything, we will feel at peace."*
> — Marianne Williamson

Ways To Start Asking

What will bring you the most happiness and self-loving thoughts?

- Ask Your Angel to help you find the humor in a situation.
- Ask Your Angel to help you find that light and that voice within.
- Ask Your Angel to help you speak kindly to yourself.
- Ask Your Angel to bring in more joy and happiness.
- Ask Your Angel to help you take the actions that will help you feel more fulfilled.

Repetition, Repetition, Repetition...

Remember, Remember, Remember… **Angels are Messengers, here to help you.**

They are here to give you what you ask for!

All you have to do is ASK!

START RIGHT NOW; not tomorrow.

Start now, and start small… it will get easier!

 "You don't have to be great to start, but you have to start to be great." — Zig Ziglar

 "Illness is the night side of life, a more onerous citizenship. Everyone who is born holds dual citizenship, in the kingdom of the well and in the kingdom of the sick." — Susan Sontag

What if I'm sick?

Being sick changes everything.

Almost everyone goes through some sort of sickness in this mortal coil called life, and as it seems these days, we all know someone who's going through a very difficult illness.

> **When you practice asking Your Angel for help and guidance regularly, you will remember to also seek her assistance when you are not feeling well.**

Sometimes, it may feel difficult to ask for help. Pain, uncertainty, loss of control, and the changes that illness brings can make it challenging to reach out. But when you have a consistent connection with Your Angel, you can release any hesitations and find it natural to ask for her assistance in your moments of need.

It's important to acknowledge that feeling negative or struggling with maintaining positivity during an injury or illness is a common and understandable response. Taking care of yourself, and seeking support from loved ones, professionals, and Your Angel is essential. In your quest for a positive mindset, you can find solace in small moments of joy, practice self-compassion, cultivate gratitude amidst challenges, and develop effective coping skills.

By nurturing a habit of seeking Your Angels' help, you create a natural inclination to turn to her even when you are unwell.

Yes, even in times of sickness, you can call upon Your Angel for help. You can ask her to just be there with you, like a friend to keep you company.

Staying positive while dealing with long-term or acute illness is indeed challenging, but there are strategies that can assist you:

Acceptance: By acknowledging and accepting your current health condition, you open the door to healing. Acceptance does not mean giving up, but rather understanding that it's okay to experience a range of emotions while taking steps towards managing your health.

I often say this to myself in times when I need acceptance:

Regret is a waste of time and I've wasted there many times.

To me, this reminds me of all the times I've spent in regret and how dwelling on those moments didn't actually make me feel any better. In fact, it made me feel worse. I say this to myself as a reminder to let go, to accept my humanity, to acknowledge that I make mistakes, miss out on things, and sometimes do things that later seem foolish and have consequences. I try to constantly remind myself that life is not about perfection; it's about experimentation.

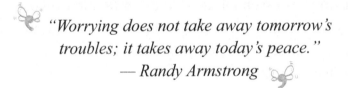

"Worrying does not take away tomorrow's troubles; it takes away today's peace."
— Randy Armstrong

Self-Care: Prioritizing self-care activities that nurture both your physical and emotional well-being is crucial. This includes rest, nourishing foods, gentle movements if possible, relaxation techniques, and engaging in activities that bring you joy and comfort.

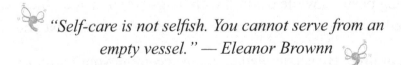

"Self-care is not selfish. You cannot serve from an empty vessel." — Eleanor Brownn

Seek Support: Reaching out to loved ones, friends, or support groups can provide you with understanding, empathy, and encouragement. Sharing your feelings and experiences with others who are going through similar challenges helps alleviate feelings of isolation.

This whole book is about seeking support, and you can always, always, always ask Your Angel for support at any time.

Focus On What You Can Control: While you may not have control over your illness, there are aspects within your control. By directing your energy towards managing symptoms, following healthcare provider recommendations, and making healthy lifestyle choices, you can support your overall well-being.

> *"You cannot control what happens to you, but you can control your attitude toward what happens to you, and in that, you will be mastering change rather than allowing it to master you."*
> *— Brian Tracy*

Set Realistic Goals: Adjusting your expectations and setting realistic goals allows you to celebrate small victories along the way. Recognizing and celebrating achievements, no matter how small, helps maintain a positive outlook.

> *"When we long for life without difficulties, remind us that oaks grow strong in contrary winds and diamonds are made under pressure."*
> *— Peter Marshall*

Practice Mindfulness & Gratitude: Cultivating mindfulness by staying present and focusing on the positive aspects of your life, even amidst challenges, is transformative. Practicing gratitude and appreciating the small blessings or moments of joy helps shift your mindset.

Engage In Activities You Enjoy: Discovering and engaging in activities that bring you happiness becomes essential. Hobbies, creative pursuits, reading, listening to music, watching uplifting movies or comedians, or engaging in activities that uplift your mood can provide comfort and healing.

"Set goals that make you want to jump out of bed in the morning, even when dealing with illness."
— *Karen Salmansohn*

Seek Professional Help If Needed: If dealing with the emotional impact of illness becomes overwhelming, seeking support from a mental health professional can provide guidance, coping strategies, and a safe space for exploration and healing. Rapid Transformational Hypnotherapy is especially helpful to naturally shift your mindset no matter what your condition is and if you would like to reach out I welcome you to schedule a 1:1 discovery call to see what Rapid Transformational Hypnotherapy or creativity coaching can do for you. You can find my calendar at **www.NicoleWhiteWellness.com**

It's important to remember that the journey with illness encompasses ups and downs. Be patient and kind with yourself, allowing the full range of emotions to be experienced.

By embracing these strategies and seeking support from Your Angel, you can foster a kinder mindset and improve your overall sense of well-being.

> *"Your beliefs and thoughts are wired into your biology. They become your cells, tissues, and organs. There's no supplement, no diet, no medicine, and no exercise regimen that can compare with the power of your thoughts and beliefs. That's the very first place you need to look when anything goes wrong with your body."*
> *— Dr. Christiane Northup*

This chapter emphasizes the importance of seeking help from Your Angel when feeling unwell.

It acknowledges the challenges of maintaining a positive mindset during illness, such as physical discomfort, emotional impact, and loss of control.

Strategies for staying positive include acceptance, self-care, seeking support, focusing on what can be controlled, setting realistic goals, practicing mindfulness and gratitude, engaging in enjoyable activities, and seeking professional help if needed.

What if... I set realistic goals based on how I'm feeling today?

Dear Angel of Healing, please help me heal my mind, body, and soul. Please watch over me, sit with me, and be my companion. Assist me in being grateful for what I do have and feeling healthy, happy, and fulfilled... or something better! Thank you, thank you, thank you.

WHEN YOU WISH UPON A STAR

Creative Practice

Art Journal Visioning:

- Write down, draw, or cut out a picture of what you wish for. Keep it close by, and keep asking Your Angel about what you need to do to receive it.

- Feel the connection with Your Angel as you ask for what you want and explore the action steps available for you.

Let's sail over to the next chapter… it's time to dock, let's anchor and remember to remember…

As far as I can tell, it's just about letting the universe know what you want and then working toward it while letting go of how it comes to pass.

— *Jim Carrey*

Chapter 25

Remember To Remember

Anchoring In Your Angel's Wisdom

How can I make it easier to put some of these tools into action?

Remember To Remember

When was the last time you sat in your car at a red light or in traffic or waited in a long line at the store, and allowed yourself to truly be present in that moment?

When out in the bustling world, running errands amidst the stress and anxiety that used to take the driver's seat, I now carry a gentle reminder that sits in my pocket. A small rock that serves as a tangible anchor—a symbol of remembering My Angel, and of the process of letting go of what is out of my control, and focusing more on what I can control… myself and my reactions.

In the past, I used to feel overwhelmed during errand days at stores, wishing everything would move faster so I could complete my tasks and return home. I would rely on distracting apps on my phone, only to realize they were robbing me of the precious moments that used to be a normal part of "being in line." **Now, whether in a store or amidst the chaos of life, my hand instinctively finds the rock in my pocket. I take a deep breath, holding the rock, feeling its weight and texture. In that moment, time slows down, and the worries that once consumed my mind can fade away. I find that I can be present, even within the chaos of the city.**

This rock becomes the catalyst for change. It reminds me that some things are beyond my control—the passing of time in traffic, and waiting in the checkout line. It encourages me to embrace the present, to observe and experience the act of running errands rather than rushing and trying to push through time, which only generates anxiety and fails to truly make progress.

Through this simple act of engaging with my anchor, this rock in my pocket, I find peace. I allow myself to pause, appreciate the world around me, and be present in the current moment, rather than thinking things should be moving faster or that I have control over those external factors. I let go of all that and embrace the present.

When was the last time you sat in your car at a red light or in traffic or waited in a long line at the store, and allowed yourself to truly be present in that moment? To feel your toes wiggling in your shoes, to feel the fabric of your clothes against your skin, to take in the motion and movement around you, to notice other people and maybe even catch eyes with someone else and exchange a friendly smile? These are the moments to savor, to be fully present. **This is meditation in everyday waking life.**

Meditation is not limited to what you do on a cushion; it extends far beyond that. It is a practice that encompasses every moment of your day-to-day life. Whether you find yourself in traffic, waiting in line, or engaged in mundane tasks, meditation invites you to cultivate a state of mindful awareness and presence. **It is in these seemingly ordinary moments that you have the opportunity to deepen your connection with the present moment, to observe your thoughts and emotions without judgment, and to bring a sense of calm and clarity to your experiences.** By integrating your anchor (rock, trinket, etc…) as a form of meditation into your daily life, you unlock the potential for greater peace, mindfulness, self-kindness, and self-discovery, transforming even the simplest of activities into opportunities for growth and inner exploration.

With my anchor and the act of engaging with it, I take a breath, release any previous stresses, and refocus my attention on what I do want—a feeling of ease and presence that assures me I'm right where I need to be in this moment.

This rock, this steadfast companion, becomes an anchor in the storm, **reminding me that I have the power to find peace within myself amidst the chaos of everyday life.** Anchors have become an essential part of the work I do to help myself and others.

An anchor awakens your senses—sight, sound, touch, taste, smell, sensation—to remind you to remember a shift in thought or action that will benefit you. **An anchor enhances**

your focus, allowing you to remain fully present in the moment. By grounding yourself with an anchor, you minimize distractions and direct your attention to the task at hand, boosting creativity, productivity, and effectiveness.

In times when anxiety threatens to overwhelm you, an anchor can be a soothing tool to ease your mind. By associating an anchor with a sense of calmness or relaxation, you can redirect your focus from anxiety to a state of inner peace and serenity in just moments.

Your mind is trainable, and the more you engage in this practice, the easier it becomes. The more you connect with your anchors, the more remarkable they become as tools in your toolbox.

Most of us live on autopilot for a good portion of the day, and anchoring yourself is at the essence of breaking free from that continual unconscious state. This entire book is about anchoring in how to Find and Communicate with Your Angel.

You can make this a mindful ritual, and having something physical as a reminder is an extremely effective way to anchor in the information you want to remain reminded of.

It's important to choose a reminder or anchor that keeps mindfulness practices and your connection with Your Angel in mind. You can use objects you come into contact with frequently—a piece of jewelry, a screensaver on your phone or computer, a rock in your pocket—or even assign significance to a particular color, so every time you see it, you pause and think about Your Angel and what you wish to anchor in.

My recent favorite way to anchor in my reminders is by choosing a song each day. I sing it in my head or out loud, playing it to tune into My Angel. I am grateful for all she provides me with, and I maintain the belief that she wants the best for me and is always there to listen and converse with me.

> **How Do You Choose To Be Reminded?**
>
> **Pick the method that resonates most with you or create your own to keep Your Angel with you at all times.**

 "You are ready and able to do beautiful things in this world, and as you walk through those doors today, you will only have two choices: love or fear. Choose love, and don't ever let fear turn you against your playful heart." — Jim Carrey

Ways To Create An Anchor

Rock (or trinket) In Your Pocket:

I often carry a little rock or crystal in my pocket as a way to remind myself to stay grounded, especially when I'm out and about running errands. You can choose any physical object that works for you, just remember to interact with it. When you do come in contact with it, take a breath and remind yourself to remember what it is that object was meant to remind you of.

The Shake It Off Method:

Shaking is truly one of my favorite ways to release negative energy and to cultivate calm, grounding, and feeling centered again. Shaking is an Anchor because you are remembering to shake off any emotions or stored-up tension or trauma that no longer serve you, therefore letting you move throughout your day with more ease, focus, and grounding.

Music:

Pick a song and set it to a reminder such as an alarm, phone, or message tone as a way to play it often and remind yourself about the messages or anchoring you attach to that song. Pick a song that makes you feel happy, or that helps you focus on what you do want.

"When you wake up with a song stuck in your head, it means an angel sang you to sleep."
— Denise Baer

Humor:

Ask yourself… how is this funny or how could this be funny in the future?

- Funny Saying or Meme.
- A song that brings in that sense of lightness and humor.
- Remember a funny joke or something a comedian said.
- Laughter Yoga, laugh for no reason.

Laughter truly is the best way to feel good instantly!

> **An anchor is anything you want it to be from sights, sounds, textures, tastes, smells, or sensations. It is a powerful tool to help you call in the assistance from Your Angel and to bring in mindfulness and focus into your daily life.**

Just as an anchor secures a ship in a storm, your anchor serves as a reminder to pause, breathe, and redirect your focus to what it is you truly want in your life… it's another way to find and invite in Your Angel.

> *"A leaf fluttered in through the window this morning, as if supported by the rays of the sun, a bird settled on the fire escape, joy in the task of coffee, joy accompanied me as I walked."*
> — Anais Nin

In this final chapter, remember the importance of remembering to remember and integrating Your Angel's wisdom into your daily life. We discussed the concept of anchors, tangible reminders that help you stay present and focused on what you desire. Examples of anchors include carrying a small rock, assigning significance to a particular color, choosing a daily song, or anything that you feel is a powerful and positive anchor for you. By utilizing anchors, you can break free from autopilot, minimize distractions, and cultivate a sense of inner peace and focus.

What if... I kept a little trinket with me today, allowing it to serve as an anchor reminding me of My Angel and to stay focused on what I truly desire?

Dear Angel of Anchors, be my guiding light and my grounding strength. Remind me of your presence day and night, and guide me to take the necessary actions to maintain and strengthen our connection together... or something better! Thank you, thank you, thank you.

REMEMBER TO REMEMBER

Anchor Doodling:

- Write out or draw an anchor you have and/or wish to get for yourself in the future, such as a rock, crystal, or trinket that means something to you.

- Write out some of the things you want this Anchor to do for you when you come in contact with it multiple times a day.

- Write out how you will remember to remember to interact and then set that as an action for your day. Do you want to carry it around with you, do you want to set an alarm to remind you… Go ahead write it out, make it real!

What a journey it's been! Come on over to the final chapter, as I want to share something with you that is near and dear to my heart and the Mission of Finding Your Angel…

Alone, we can do so little; together, we can do so much.

— *Helen Keller*

Chapter 26

Stone Soup

The Transformative Power Of Community

Why is community so essential to health and wellness?

Stone Soup

Our tale takes place in a little village where a weary and hungry traveler arrives with nothing but an empty cooking pot. Much like the timeless fable of Stone Soup, the locals are hesitant to share their precious food with the hungry stranger.

Undeterred, the traveler walks down to a nearby stream, starts a campfire, and fills the pot with water and a peculiar stone. A villager watches this stranger with suspicion and shares this with another villager.

The villager then approaches the traveler with a mind full of wonder and curiosity about what is going on. "Why are you boiling that stone?" Asks the villager. Well, with mischief in her eyes, the traveler reveals that this is no ordinary soup – it's a magical creation that, with only a few missing ingredients, could be a delectable feast for the entire village.

An open-minded villager, enticed by the promise of a shared meal, decides to contribute some of their own food to enhance the flavor. Word of this communal soup spreads through the village like wildfire, and soon, more and more villagers join in. Each villager eager to be part of the communal soup added their own ingredient – potatoes, onions, cabbage, peas, and a whole bunch more!

Finally, with everyone's contribution, the traveler declares that the stone (which was inedible) was now unnecessary and removed it. Voila! A pot of delicious soup emerged, filling the air with mouthwatering aroma.

The traveler now smiles as she scoops out the soup to each of the villagers and then sits with her own, enjoying the soup, knowing that she too has brought this community together while also filling her hungry belly.

Echoing in the spirit of Stone Soup, where a simple stone transforms into a savory meal through it's collective efforts of the community, our story unfolds. It stands as a heartwarming importance to the extraordinary potential that emerges when people come together, pooling their resources and talents to create something far more enriching than any
single contribution.

The magic of sharing and collaboration transforms a simple stone into a delicious feast, reminding us of the power of community, generosity, and creativity!

When The World Changes

In 2020, we all faced a surprising challenge that disrupted our lives and the way we connect. Isolation became the right thing to do, and the value and loss of community became more evident than ever. The absence of in-person interactions left a huge void, making me realize the importance of our need for human connection and community.

Online communities have become a lifeline, and while they don't replace face-to-face interactions, they play a crucial role in our lives. Now, it's time to strike a balance between online and offline activities for your health and emotional well-being.

Have you heard of the "Blue Zones?" These are communities around the world where people are known to live with more vitality and longevity, with many easily surpassing 100 years of age. As I researched these places, three things seemed to be consistent throughout all of these Blue Zone Communities:

- **Nutritious food:** Eating home-cooked nutritious foods.

- **Having a passion and purpose that also involves movement:** Engaging in activities such as gardening, crafts, dancing, games, cooking, etc…

- **Community:** Perhaps the most striking aspect of Blue Zones is the profound sense of community that thrives within them. People in these regions don't just coexist; they actively engage with one another. They form deep connections, supporting each other through life's challenges and celebrations. This strong sense of belonging contributes significantly to their health and wellness as a whole.

"The way you get meaning into your life is to devote yourself to loving others, devote yourself to your community around you, and devote yourself to creating something that gives you purpose and meaning." — Mitch Albom

Internet Isolation

As you're likely aware, the internet is a double-edged sword. It offers immediate access to information but also creates comparison, unhappiness, and disconnection. Many people today, whether consciously or not, prioritize online interactions over real-life relationships and genuine community. This can result in feelings of loneliness and detachment.

To create balance, it's essential to consciously manage your online time and prioritize hands-on creativity, community, and personal connections. It's your respons-ability to be mindful of the amount of time spent online and to consciously refocus on the real world around you.

While the events of 2020 intensified isolation and reliance on the online world, it is now your respons-ability to shift your focus to spend more time in the physical world around you. Engaging in any of the Creative Practices such as writing, drawing, painting, gardening, cooking, and crafts can provide fulfillment and help you appreciate the value and beauty of real-life connection, far more than constant online time, and it's always better with a friend or Your Angel.

Here are some offline activities that offer significant benefits:

- **During meals:** Write, doodle, gaze out a window, or engage in a conversation with someone instead of scrolling or watching something on a screen. I've learned over the years that meals are much more satisfying when enjoyed without screens or distractions.

- **Find reasons to go outside:** Having a dog is a surefire way to get outdoors at least four to five times a day. Even in inclement weather, taking a few minutes outside is essential. Visit a park, garden or join a community garden, take a drive, or simply go for a walk. Stepping outside into the natural world provides a refreshing change that we all need.

- **An hour before bedtime:** Turn off all electronic devices, such as your phone, television, or tablet. Instead, read a physical book, journal, art journal, write to Your Angel, or engage in any of the creative practices mentioned throughout the book. The blue light emitted by your gadgets can interfere with your natural ability to fall asleep and enjoy a good night's rest.

- **In the morning:** Dedicate time to journaling, venture outside, prepare your favorite morning beverage, and let your morning be yours. Resist the urge to interact online, or read the news first thing in the morning. See what it feels like to have your own thoughts and journal or art journal about them. Connect with Your Angel first thing in the morning, this sets a lovely tone and connection to your day.

It's important to establish clear boundaries with your electronic devices. Being tethered to them around the clock is neither healthy nor conducive to genuine connection. Schedule time during your day when you are doing real-life activities and can step away from all gadgets, instead use time each day to engage in some of the Creative Practices, connect with Family, Friends, and of course Your Angel!

> **I have found it difficult to truly connect with My Angel when I'm on a gadget… to me, she is a real-life connection that requires focus to talk to her and to write to her. I find it's more powerful with pen and paper than on a keyboard.**

In 2020, I closed my office and moved to the telecommuting world. While it's not the ideal scenario, it has broadened our horizons, allowing us to include people from all over the map. We've adapted by creating an online space that fosters real-life activities. We draw, paint, doodle, journal, and share together. People have even formed friendships and in-person get-togethers from our community as well. Often there is a prompt given and then we use the Live/Online class time to share our thoughts, insights, and Creative Practices.

The Transformative Power Of Community

Community is vital for health and wellness, just like the vibrant "Blue Zones." It reduces stress, combats loneliness, and fills your life with a sense of purpose and happiness.

In essence, community nurtures you, offering valuable support, and enhancing the quality of your life.

> *"There is no power for change greater than a community discovering what it cares about."*
> *— Margaret J. Wheatley*

In closing, I want to remind you of the incredible journey you've traveled on. You've explored the possibilities of your creativity, found a deeper connection with yourself, and learned how to enhance your well-being by connecting with Your Angel. As you've discovered, the power of community and the sense of belonging are essential in your life.

Remember the timeless wisdom of "Stone Soup." May your hearts be stirred by the magic that unfolds when hands and community unite in the shared joy of creating something wonderful together! Your Community looks forward to welcoming you with open arms and witnessing your Transformational Creativity. Thank you for being a part of this journey. The best is yet to come!

What if... I looked for ways that I am connected to community and cultivated those relationships even more?

Dear Angel of Community, please guide me to finding and creating a community that will help me age with grace, passion, connection, health, and purpose, or something better... Thank you, thank you, thank you!

Community Doodle:

- Envision your ideal community. Doodle or Write about what values, activities, and connections are essential to create the ideal community for you?

- How would this community contribute to your creativity, connection, and wellness?

- What would your roles be within the community, what will you contribute?

- What real-life activities bring you joy?

- How do you balance online and offline time? What helps you stay connected to hands-on creativity and community?

You did it! You made it through this Finding Your Angel and Transformational Creativity Book! Did you find what you were looking for? Do you want your journey to continue with a creative and transformational community? If so, turn the page as I invite you to continue your self-enrichment with like-minded friends.

www.NicoleWhiteWellness.com

One Last Message

"Cherish your visions.
Cherish your ideals.
Cherish the music that stirs in your heart,
the beauty that forms in your mind,
the loveliness that drapes your purest thoughts.
For out of them will grow all delightful conditions,
all heavenly environment,
of these, if you but remain true to them,
your world will at last be built."

— *James Allen*
As a Man Thinketh

Thank you for joining us on this Creative and Transformative Journey to Finding Your Angel. Remember that creativity is a space and place that calls for specific action — the action of creating repeatedly. Create your space, and that space will seemingly begin to create for you. No matter how big or small, from a sketchbook to a studio, energetically enhance your space by engaging in creative practices daily.

So... what will you take with you to help during troubled times?

What resonated with you in this Finding Your Angel book?

Do you feel that there are more opportunities for connection and messages from Your Angel?

You now stand on the spiritual shoulders of centuries, believing and interacting with Angels and the love and messages they gift to you. Let Your Angel bring you messages of comfort, healing, creativity, empowerment, and transformation!

Let Your Angel be by your side, let her be that bright light that holds you, helps you, encourages you, and guides you to your true path, your true being.

The Ending Is Just The Beginning.

I invite you to reach out and check out our online Creative Community! There are free resources and opportunities to join us Live/Online. Please visit www.NicoleWhiteWellness.com for more information.

**Tell me and I forget.
Teach me and I remember.
Involve me and I learn.**
— *Benjamin Franklin*

Remember to listen closely,
Your Angel always has
a message for you!

To You & Your Angel!

Love, Nicole

"Hope" is the thing
With feathers
That perches in the soul
And sings the tune
Without the words
And never stops - at all.

— Emily Dickinson

Acknowledgments

Thank you, Thank You, Thank You, I hope you all know what you mean to me and the place in my heart you hold.

Alyssa S., Ava & Yeshua O., Avi S., Ayu O., Brenda E., Bridgette W., Cambria M., Caren W., Charlie & Laura B., Charlie C., Cyn L., Dad, Denise B., Denise D., Dewey T., Elaine H., Eleanore W., Eric T., Erin B., Gabbie W., Georges C., Gina B., Greg D., Gypsy Raven, Hannah W., Ina C., Isaiah W., Jacob W., Jane Z., Jean S., Jen & Heathar, Jerry G., John & Liz B., Judith F., Julie F., Julie T., Karuna, Kat C., Katrina H., Kim H., Kim R., Kristi I., Kristin R., Leslie M., Lina R., Linda M., Linda M., Luigi D., Mallory B., Manny T., Melinda Y., Michael H., Mom, Monica A., Monica K., Monica P., Pam W., Patty S., Phebe & Mac, Ruth S., Ryan W., Sue M., Susannah W., Suzy S., Tiffani C., Tyler & Kayla, Valaluck T., Veronica L., Wade K., and Zoë Wild!

ACKNOWLEDGMENTS

Through the years, I have engaged with so many ideas, certifications, books, teachings, mentoring, and support that have greatly impacted my life. It's truly impossible to thank everyone who's taken me on their journey. I know many of you and many I hope to know in the future, some I will only know in my dreams.

Abraham & Esther Hicks, Albert Einstein, Anais Nin, Andrea Beaman, Ari Whitten, Arianna Huffington, Benjamin Hoff, Betty Edwards, Bob Ross, Bobby McFerrin, Brené Brown, Brian Johnson, Brendon Burchard, Brian Tracy, Bruce Lipton, Byron Katie, Carl Jung, Carlos Rosas, Carole King, Cloe Madanes, Colette Baron Reid, Daniel Amen, Daniel Merriam, David Gandelman, David Lynch, David R. Hawkins, Dean Graziosi, Debbie Rosas, Denise Baer, Derik Lin, Diane von Furstenberg, Don Miguel Ruiz, Donna Eden, Dr. Andrew Weil, Dr. Christiane Northrup, Dr. Joe Dispenza, Dr. Dr. Josh Axe, Dr. Joe Vitale, Dr. Mark Hyman, Dr. Seuss, Eckhart Tolle, Ed Mylett, Elizabeth Gilbert, Emily Dickinson, Gabrielle Bernstein, Gary Vaynerchuck, Georgia O'Keeffe, Gwyneth Paltrow, J.K. Rowling, James Malinchak, Jack Canfield, James Allen, Jay Shetty, Jim Carrey, Jim Kwik, Jim Rohn, John Assaraf, John Lee Dumas, Joseph Campbell, Joshua Rosenthal, Judy Blume, Julia Cameron, Kate Northrup, Keanu Reeves, Kelle Rae Oien, Kris Carr, Kurt Vonnegut, Laura Lynne Jackson, Lisa Asiago, Lisa Nichols, Louise Hay, Mastin Kipp, Marie Forleo, Marisa Peer, Mark Victor Hansen, Mark & Magali Peysha, Maya Angelou, Mel Robbins, Michael Beckwith, Michael Hyatt, Michele Cassou, Neale Donald Walsch, Nikola Tesla, Oprah Winfrey, Osho, Paulo Coelho, Pema Chödrön, Peter H. Reynolds, Radha Agrawal,

Rhonda Byrne, Rumi, Seth Apter, Seth Godin, Shel Silverstein, Simon Sinek, Stephen Hawking, Steve Maraboli, Steven Pressfield, Tim Burton, Tim Ferriss, Tony & Page Robbins, Tracy Weber, Vishen Lakhiani, Vladimir Kush, Walt Disney, Wayne W. Dyer, Weird Al Yankovic, Yoda, Zig Zigler, and all the other teachers, artists, and guides out there!

To those who are not mentioned here, the impressions you made are still in my heart.

Who's Nicole?

Nicole White is recognized as an Author, Artist, Certified Hypnotherapist, Rapid Transformational Therapist, Certified Holistic Health Coach, Strategic Intervention Coach, Registered Yoga Instructor and Educator, Course Creator, and Instructor as well as a Creative Community Builder!

My Mission is to empower you in this vibrant chapter of your life, helping you quickly unlock your creative abilities and transform for the better. My research-based approach breaks free from self-imposed limits, offering simple and fun creative practices to manage stress, release depression and anxiety, find purpose, and embrace a more fulfilling and creative life.

Nicole's Inspiration Board was featured in the magazine Where Women Create in the Fall of 2022

Nicole was the owner of Raven Art Center and appeared multiple times on KRQE 13 TV Morning Show in Albuquerque, NM

Nicole's Raven Art Center was a featured article in Albuquerque's Weekly Magazine, The Alibi

Collaborative Mural Project with Coral Community School

Nicole has delivered over 500 presentations both online and in person for The University of New Mexico since 2011.

Nicole can speak for groups ranging from 10 – 20,000

www.NicoleWhiteWellness.com

Index

A

Abraham Hicks 78
A Brain, A Heart,
    And Courage 63
A Bucchianeri 96
Acceptance 274
accomplishment 81
Acknowledgments 304
Action vs. Acceptance 163
ADDITIONAL RESOURCES 318
Adopting A Beginner's Mind 42
Albert Einstein 33, 67
all-or-nothing 28
Alone 129
A Message To You xx
Am I enough 237
Anais Nin 287
anchor 283
Anchor Doodling 289
Anchoring In Your Angel's Wisdom
    281
Angel Art Doodle 243, 253
Angel Art Journaling 258, 259, 261
Angel Clarence 101
Angel Doodle 7
Angelic Beings 3
Angels are always listening and waiting
    for you to ask 105
Angels Are Always Present 1
Angels are messengers 4
Angels are Messengers 272
Angel Trick 122
Angel Writing 226
Angel Writing Exploration 233
anxiety 75
Aretha Franklin 132
Arianna Huffington 32
artistic excellence 112
Art Journal 256

Art Journaling 256, 261
Art Journaling Is
    An Anything-Goes Process 255
Art Journal Visioning 265, 279
art supplies 77
Art Therapeutics ix
ART THERAPEUTICS Live/Online
    Courses 318
Ask 18
ASK 3, 12, 22, 95
Ask & Action Method 268
Ask for the solution 103
Asking 196
Asking Your Angel Practice 219
ask Your Angel 66
Ask Your Angel 105
ask Your Angel for help 103

B

Becoming Solution Oriented 9
beginner's mind 50, 72
Beginner's Mind 43
beginner's mindset 44
belief 2, 13, 17, 23
Belief Doodle 15
Belief Like A Child 193
Belief Like A Feather 9
belief systems 172
Believe 22
benefits 209, 295
Benjamin Franklin 302
Benjamin Hoff 21
best friend 11
be-you-tiful 71
black-or-white 28
BLACK & WHITE THINKING 34
Blue Zones 293, 297
Bobbie McFerrin 207
Bob Hope 152

Bob Ross 151
break free 174
Breaking Free 89
breaking free from the victim mindset 229
Breathe deeply 115
Breathing Exercises 204
Brené Brown 204
Brian Johnson 49
Brianna Wiest 88
Brian Tracy 275
Bring in Your Angel,
 and ask her to help you! 135
Bruce Lee 128
butterfly 169
Byron Katie 131, 230
Byron Pulsifer 150

C

Carl Jung 62
Carole King 203
Catching the Big Fish 111
caterpillar 169
Change doesn't happen by complaining 163
change those old stories 176
Changing The All-Or-Nothing Mindset 31
childhood dreams 59
childhood experience 171
Cleaning 204
Cloud-Ish 202
Communicating with Your Angel 197
Community 293, 297
Community Doodle 299
Comparison Is A Terrible Torture! 83
compassionate 36
complaining 82
compliment 122
Compliment Giver 122
compliment-rejecting mind 122
Confucius 32
connection 74

Cooking 204
coping skills 273
Craig D. Lounsbrough 188
Creating An Inspiration Wall 248
Creating Belief 195
Creating Compassionate Self-Talk 129
creative abilities 152
creative actions 246
creative expression 112
creative journey 72
creative outlets 73
creative practice 203
Creative Practice 5, 84, 256
Creative Practice Part I 71
Creative Practice Part II 201
Creative Practice Part III 213
Creative Practice Part IV 235
Creative Practice Part V 245
Creative Practice Part VI 255
Creative Practices 24, 74, 75, 208
creativity 75
Creativity — Like A Dance 245
cultivate curiosity 50
Cupid 3
Curiosità 41, 49, 50, 247
Curiosità Doodling 53
curiosity 44

D

David Allen 37
David Lynch 83, 111, 112, 113, 124, 224
Dear Angel 5, 135, 138, 140
Dear Angel of Anchors 288
Dear Angel of Artistic Expressions, please 210
Dear Angel of Art Journaling 264
Dear Angel of Belief 14
Dear Angel of Communication 198
Dear Angel of Community 298
Dear Angel of Curiosity 52
Dear Angel of Flexibility 38
Dear Angel of Focus 86

Dear Angel of Healing 278
Dear Angel of Humor 156
Dear Angel of Imagination 242
Dear Angel of Inner Guidance 60
Dear Angel of Inspiration 252
Dear Angel of Mindfulness 126
Dear Angel of New Beginnings 178
Dear Angel of Peace 24
Dear Angel of Responsiveness 190
Dear Angel of Self-Compassion 146
Dear Angel of Self-Discovery 68
Dear Angel of Solutions 98, 108
Dear Angel of the Unknown 166
Dear Angel of Transformation 76
Dear Angel of Writing 232
Dear Art Angel 255
Dear Guardian Angel 6
Debbie Rosas 248
Dedication xvi
depression 74, 75
Diane von Furstenberg 141
discover what does work for you 64
discover what works for you 29
Does It Have To Be All-Or-Nothing? 27
Don Miguel Ruiz 95
Donna Eden 236
Don't Throw The Baby Out With The Bathwater 161
Doodle-ISH 211
Dorothy 63
Dot Doodles 77
Drawing 77
Drawing or Doodling 205
Dr. Christiane Northup 250, 254, 277
Dr. Daniel Amen 91
reams 57
Dr. Seuss 66
Dumbo 9, 13

E

Eckhart Tolle 110, 180
Eileen Elias Freeman xxii

Elizabeth Gilbert 209
Elizabeth King 67
Embrace Flexibility 35
Embrace The Gray Areas 34
Embracing Change And Transformation 169
Emily Dickinson 303
epiphany 27, 80
expecting others to change 82
Explore The Possibilities 47
Expressing Emotions 260

F

Fear of Failure 31
Fiber Arts 206
Finding Funny 149
Finding The Middle Ground 27
Finding Your Angel Doodle 25
Finding yourself 29
Finding Your Way 55
flexibility 37
focus 95
Focus 43
FOCUS 103
focusing on the solution 97
Focusing On What You Do Want 82
Focusing On Your Strengths 139
Focus on what you can control 96
Focus On What You Can Control 275
focus, repetition 37
For Calling On Your Angel? 22
fresh perspective 43
fulfillment 75, 76

G

Gardening 205
George Carlin 153
George Eliot 59
Georgia O'Keeffe 70
Get Curious 49
grateful 36
Gratitude 119, 260
Gratitude & Release 260

guidance 3

H

habit 19
habitual patterns 174
Harry Potter 13
Have You Been Searching...
 Searching For Something? 64
Having a passion and purpose 293
healing 74
healing journey 258
Helen Keller 290
Hope i
How can I be open to the idea that it's possible
 to communicate with My Angel? 193
How do Angels communicate? 154
How To Communicate With Your Angel 196
How To Focus On The Solution? 95
Humor 149, 205, 286
Hurt people hurt people. 129
hurt people tend to hurt people 133
Hypnotherapist xv
hypnotherapy 27
Hypnotherapy vi
hypnotic states 174

I

I AM ENOUGH 132
Illuminated Doodles 69
infinite creativity 82
Inner Journey Doodle 191
inner voice 55
inspirational items 249
Inspiration Wall 250
Internet Isolation 294
Interrupting The Hypnotic State 173
inventors 134
ISH 201
I Think I Can 17
It's a Wonderful Life 101

It's A Wonderful Life 101
I wonder 45
I Wonder 51
I Wonder... 44

J

Jack Canfield 19, 183, 269
James Allen 301
Jim Carrey 30, 280
Jim Kwik 11, 133
Jim Rohn 184
JK Rowling 10
John Assaraf 8, 92, 137, 270
John F. Kennedy 32
Johnny Cash 32
John Wooden 23
Joseph Campbell 261
Joseph Wood Krutch 104
journaling 97
joy 74
Julia Cameron 73, 75, 224, 226
Just Some Of The Creative Practices 204

K

Karen Borga 104
Karen Salmansohn 276
Keanu Reeves 244
Kris Carr 234
Kurt Vonnegut 154

L

Lady In White 193
Lao Tzu 106, 188
Laughter Doodle 157
Laughter Yoga 149
Laura Lynne Jackson 197
Les Brown 212
Letting Go Doodle 167
Letting Go Of Expectations
 And Embracing The Unknown 159

Lilly & The Angel 213
Listening 56
listen to yourself 55
Looking Within 63
Louise Hay 16, 134, 144

M

Madeleine L'Engle 195
Magical 269
Margaret J. Wheatley 297
Marianne Williamson 271
Marie Forleo 20, 241
Marisa Peer 36, 93, 132, 143
Mark Twain 148, 186
Mark Victor Hansen 270
Martin Luther King, Jr. 107
Mary Jac 100
Mastering The Art Of Asking 101, 104, 268
Maya Angelou 33, 138
meditation 112, 124
Meditation 197
Meditation In A Strange Place 111
Melanie Beckler 223
mental and physical relief 74
mental illness 73
messengers 2
Metamorphosis 169
Mia Hamm 33
Michael Jordan 33
Michelangelo xxxii
mindfulness 112
Mindfulness And Shaking It Off 111
Mindfulness Doodle 127
mindfulness practices 124
Mirroring 165
Mitch Albom 294
Movement 205
Moving Meditations 123
Music 286
myth of multitasking 175

N

natural creativity 77
Nature 205
navigate challenges 35
Navigating Expectations 164
Negative self-talk 135, 139
Nelson Mandela 139
Nick Bantock 200
Nikki Rowe 13
Nikola Tesla xx
Non-Dominant Hand Doodles 179
North Star Doodles 61
nourishment iii
Nutritious food 293

O

Obstacle Course 41
Old negative self-talk 137
One Last Message 301
Open Up To Embrace Curiosity 47
Oprah Winfrey 32
Osho 158
overcome self-doubt 72
Overcoming Procrastination 47
overwhelming anxiety 74

P

Pablo Picasso 82
painting 73, 77
Painting & Mixed Media 206
Panic attacks 74
PAST EXPERIENCES 34
Paulo Coelho 181, 189
PERFECTIONISM 31
Peter H. Reynolds 71, 201
Peter Marshall 275
Pets 206
Photography 206
Practice Finding Your Angel 196
Practice Mindfulness & Gratitude 276
Practicing mindfulness 113
Professional Help 276
Professional Speaker xiv
PROGRESS over PERFECTION 31

INDEX

protect myself 130
Purple-Quilly 79, 80

R

Randy Armstrong 274
Rapid Transformational Therapy (RTT) 36
Redefine Your Own Success 31
Reflecting and Curiosity 135
Reflection Doodle: 109
Reframe 136
Reframed positive thoughts 135, 137, 139
reframe your self-talk 144
re-framing 37
Reframing Negative Self-Talk 92
Release Doodle: 39
releasing his anger 112
Releasing the All-Or-Nothing Mindset 27
releasing the victim mentality 97
Remember To Remember 281
Removing The Obstacles 41
repetition 23, 24, 43
Repetition 17, 18, 19
Repetition, Repetition, Repetition 272
Respect Yourself By Speaking Compassionately To Yourself 133
Response-Ability 183
Response-Ability And Reframing Negative Thoughts 181
Robert Anthony 192
Robert Brault 36
RTT, Rapid Transformational Therapy vi
Rumi 43, 217, 266

S

Santiago 182
satisfaction 81
Saying Thank You! 120
Sean Stephenson 140
Seeking Help From Your Angel When Feeling Unwell 267
Seek Support 275
Self-Compassion 34
Self-criticism is downright hazardous to your health! 132
Self-criticism is one of the biggest forms of stress, anxiety, and depression 132
self-discovery 64, 74, 75
self-esteem 133
self-exploration 112
self-expression 76
Selfie Doodle 147
self-talk 134
sense of humor 152
sense of purpose 74
Seth Apter 247
Set Realistic Goals 275
Shake it Off 124
Shaking 118
Shifting Your Focus To What You DO Want 79
SHIFT your focus to ASKING for a SOLUTION 104
Shunryu Suzuki 40
Signs & Symbols 197
Simon Sinek 26
Simple Breathing Techniques 116
simplicity 112
Singing 206
Small accomplishment 37
Small Steps = Strong Habits 186
Societal & Cultural Influences 34
softening my self-talk 131
Solution 12, 22, 103, 215
Solution Doodling 99
Some Names You Can Call Your Angel 21
So… What Are Angels? 10
Special FREE Bonus Gift For You 318
SQUIRREL 80
Squirrel-Itis 79

Squirrel-itis Doodle 87
starry sky 268
starting small 72
Start Small 45
Stephen Hawking 216
Steve Maraboli 176
Steve Mehr 223
Stone Soup 291, 297
Stop being a victim 89
stressful 118, 124
Struggling to receive compliments? 121
Susan Sontag 272
Symbolic Serendipities Doodle 199

T

Take Action 18, 22, 188
Take A Deep Breath 114
Tesla 134
Thank You, Thank You, Thank You 23
The Alchemist 181
The Angel Doll 235
The Ant and the Grasshopper 79
The Ask & Action Method 106
The Benefits Of Humor 149
The Dot 71, 72, 73
The Ending Is Just The Beginning 302
The Gifts And Messages From Your Angel 1
The Gifts of Angels 3
The Importance Of "Yet" 142
The Little Engine That Could 17
The Magic Of Saying "Thank You." 121
The Mission xix
The Origins Of Angels 1
The Pink Panther 162
The Power Of: Or Something Better 163
There Is A Voice Inside Of You 55
The Secret Sauce 129
The Secret To Calling In Your Angel 20
the secret you have been looking for 65
The Shake It Off Method 117, 286
the solution 41
The Transformative Power Of Community 297
The Transformative Power Of Community 291
the transformative power of connection and community 102
the transformative power of self-compassion 144
the universe 58
the way you speak to yourself 91
The Wise Farmer 159
The Wizard of Oz 64, 67
the zone 246
Thomas Edison 33
those dreams were not random whispers 57
Tim Burton 57
time for a change 131
Timothy Shriver 196
To download your Meditation 113
Tony Robbins 41, 42, 161
train people how to treat you 123
Transformation 170
TRANSFORMATIONAL 269
Transformational Asking! 268
Transformational Creativity 297
Transformational Creativity Book 299
Transformational Creativity Coach xv
Transformational Creativity Revolution xix
transformative power 3
Travel & Adventure 207
Treating Yourself With Kindness And Understanding 137
True Purpose 76

U

Understanding Expectations 161
understanding of yourself 74

Understanding What You Can And Can't Control 89
Understanding What You Can & Can't Control 93
understand who YOU 29
unrealistic expectations 202
Upgradeology, Upgrade Your Food, Upgrade Your Life 75
Using Repetition To Get What You Want 17
Using The Creative Practice Part II 203

V

Vincent Van Gogh 83

W

wake-up call 91, 130
Walt Disney 10
Ways To Become Response-Able 185
Ways To Create An Anchor 285
What Do I Call My Angel? 20
What Do You Wish For? 223
What if 6–318, 24, 38, 52, 60, 68, 76, 86, 98, 108, 126, 146, 156, 166, 178, 190, 198, 210, 232, 242, 252, 264, 278, 288, 298
What if I'm sick? 272
What is Essential to Believe? 12
What Is The Formula 22
What is the solution? 96
What Others Are Saying iii–318
What The Creative Practices Can Do For You 73
What The Creative Practices Have Done For Me 74
What Will You Ask Of Your Angel? 223
What You CAN Control 93
What You CAN'T Control 94
When The World Changes 293
When You Wish Upon A Sta 267

Where Women Create 247
whispers of your own heart and soul. 56
Who's Nicole? 307
Why Believe? 11
William Shakespeare 20
Winston Churchill 35
wonder 268
writing 73
Writing 74, 197, 207, 225
Writing & Speaking Out Loud 215

Y

The Power of YET 146, 187
Yoda xxii
Yogi Bhajan 183
You Are What You Put In Or Allow In Your Atmosphere 151
You CAN Paint ix, 71, 202, 206
You CAN Paint! Live/Online Courses 318
you don't have to look the part to play the part you want 125
Your Angel & Repetition 18
Your Angel WANTS to answer you 46
Your attention is a compass 42
your authentic path 57
Your Inner Path 58
your meditation download 125
You Were Born An Artist 82

Z

Zen Proverb 102
Zig Ziglar 19, 272

NOTES

www.NicoleWhiteWellness.com

ADDITIONAL RESOURCES

You CAN Paint! Live/Online Courses

ART THERAPEUTICS Live/Online Courses

Special FREE Bonus Gift For You

To help you achieve more success, there are **FREE BONUS RESOURCES** for you at:
www.NicoleWhiteWellness.com

Made in the USA
Monee, IL
27 January 2024